Ninja Creami
Cookbook
2023

1500 Days Easy and Tasty Ice Cream, Gelato, Sorbet, Ice Cream Mixins Recipes for Beginners to Master Your New Machine

Albert S. Gibson

Copyright© 2022 By Albert S. Gibson

All rights reserved worldwide.

No part of this book may be reproduced or transmitted in any form or by any means, electronic or mechanical, including photo- copying, recording or by any information storage and retrieval system, without written permission from the publisher, except for the inclusion of brief quotations in a review.

Warning-Disclaimer

The purpose of this book is to educate and entertain. The author or publisher does not guarantee that anyone following the techniques, suggestions, tips, ideas, or strategies will become successful. The author and publisher shall have neither liability or responsibility to anyone with respect to any loss or damage caused, or alleged to be caused, directly or indirectly by the information contained in this book.

Table of Contents

INTRODUCTION 1

Chapter 2 Ice Cream Mix-ins 2

Chapter 2 Ice Cream Mix-ins 6

Chocolate Brownie Ice Cream 7	Coffee Chip Ice Cream 10
Rocky Road Ice Cream 7	Sweet Potato Pie Ice Cream 10
Bourbon-maple-walnut Ice Cream 7	Vanilla Ice Cream With Chocolate Chips 11
Pistachio Ice Cream 8	Lavender Cookie Ice Cream 11
Sneaky Mint Chip Ice Cream 8	Coconut Mint Chip Ice Cream 11
Birthday Cake Ice Cream 8	Jelly & Peanut Butter Ice Cream 11
Grasshopper Ice Cream 9	Triple-chocolate Ice Cream 12
Cookies & Cream Ice Cream 9	Fruity Cereal Ice Cream 12
Coffee And Cookies Ice Cream 9	Lite Chocolate Cookie Ice Cream 12
Cookies And Coconut Ice Cream 9	Rum Raisin Ice Cream 13
Mint Chocolate Chip Ice Cream 10	Snack Mix Ice Cream 13
Mint Cookies Ice Cream 10	Lavender Cookies & Cream Ice Cream 13

Chapter 3 Ice Cream Recipes 14

Carrot Ice Cream 15	Blueberry Ice Cream 18
Classic Vanilla Ice Cream 15	Creamy Caramel Macchiato Coffee Ice Cream 18
Peanut Butter Ice Cream 15	Kale'd By Chocolate Ice Cream 19
Coffee Ice Cream 15	French Vanilla Ice Cream 19
Matcha Ice Cream 16	Super Lemon Ice Cream 19
Sea Salt Caramel Ice Cream 16	Mint Cookie Ice Cream 19
Earl Grey Tea Ice Cream 16	Chocolate Ice Cream 20
Peanut Butter & Jelly Ice Cream 16	Cinnamon Red Hot Ice Cream 20
Strawberry Ice Cream 17	Blackberry Ice Cream 20
Mocha Ice Cream 17	Mango Ice Cream 20
Pear Ice Cream 17	Lemon Ice Cream 20
Fruity Carrot Ice Cream 17	Cherry-chocolate Chunk Ice Cream 21
Low-sugar Vanilla Ice Cream 17	Chocolate & Spinach Ice Cream 21
Coconut-vanilla Ice Cream 18	Philadelphia-style Chocolate Ice Cream 21
Strawberry-carrot Ice Cream 18	Fruity Extract Ice Cream 21
Coconut Ice Cream 18	Pumpkin Gingersnap Ice Cream 22

Chapter 4 Gelato Recipes

- Cherry Gelato 24
- Cantaloupe Sorbet 24
- Orange Sherbet 24
- Triple Chocolate Gelato 24
- Banana & Squash Cookie Gelato 25
- Vanilla Gelato 25
- Chocolate Cauliflower Gelato 25
- Chocolate Hazelnut Gelato 25
- Maple Gelato 26
- Marshmallow Cookie Gelato 26
- Apple Cider Sorbet 26
- Berries Mascarpone Gelato 26
- Sweet Potato Gelato 27
- Peanut Butter Gelato 27
- Marshmallow Gelato 27
- Squash Gelato 27
- Carrot Gelato 28
- Red Velvet Gelato 28
- Pumpkin Gelato 28
- Vanilla Bean Gelato 28
- Tiramisu Gelato 29
- Blueberry & Crackers Gelato 29
- Spirulina Cookie Gelato 29
- Pecan Gelato 30
- Caramel Egg Gelato 30

Chapter 5 Smoothie Bowls Recipes

- Strawberry-orange Creme Smoothie 32
- Raspberry & Mango Smoothie Bowl 32
- Vanilla Pumpkin Pie Smoothie 32
- Pumpkin & Banana Smoothie Bowl 32
- Gator Smoothies 32
- Crazy Fruit Smoothie 33
- Kale, Avocado & Fruit Smoothie Bowl 33
- Coffee Smoothie Bowl 33
- Chocolate Pumpkin Smoothie Bowl 33
- Avocado & Banana Smoothie Bowl 33
- Green Monster Smoothie 34
- Chocolate Fudge Frosting 34
- Simple Smoothie Bowl 34
- Strawberry Smoothie Bowl 34
- Microwave Vanilla Cake 34
- Vodka Smoothie 35
- Peaches And Cream Smoothie Bowl 35
- Fruity Coffee Smoothie Bowl 35
- Buttery Coffee Smoothie 35
- Avocado Smoothie 35
- Dragon Fruit & Pineapple Smoothie Bowl ... 35
- Piescream 36
- Mixed Berries Smoothie Bowl 36
- Mango Smoothie Bowl 36
- Fruity Coconut Smoothie Bowl 36
- Oat Banana Smoothie Bowl 36
- Three Fruit Smoothie Bowl 37
- Peach & Grapefruit Smoothie Bowl 37
- Kale VS Avocado Smoothie Bowl 37
- Pumpkin Smoothie Bowl 37
- Mango & Orange Smoothie Bowl 37
- Papaya Smoothie Bowl 38
- Blueberry Smoothie Bowl 38
- Pineapple Smoothie Bowl 38
- Energy Elixir Smoothie 38
- Frozen Fruit Smoothie Bowl 38
- Raspberry Smoothie Bowl 38
- Chocolate, Peanut Butter & Banana Smoothie ... 39
- Green Fruity Smoothie Bowl 39
- Piña Smoothie Bowl 39
- Raspberry & Orange Smoothie Bowl 39
- Orange & Mango Smoothie Bowl 39
- Berries & Cherry Smoothie Bowl 40

Chapter 6 Sorbet Recipes — 41

- Coconut Lime Sorbet 42
- Cherry-berry Rosé Sorbet 42
- Celery Sorbet 42
- Strawberry Sorbet 42
- Plum Sorbet 43
- Pineapple & Rum Sorbet 43
- Peach Sorbet 43
- Raspberry Lime Sorbet 43
- Banana Sorbet 43
- Raspberry Sorbet 43
- Lemony Herb Sorbet 44
- Lime Beer Sorbet 44
- Mango Sorbet 44
- Mango Chamoy Sorbet 44
- Avocado Lime Sorbet 44
- Pear Sorbet 45
- Acai & Fruit Sorbet 45
- Cherry Sorbet 45
- Pomegranate Sorbet Smile 45
- Italian Ice Sorbet 45
- Strawberry & Beet Sorbet 46
- Strawberries & Champagne Sorbet 46
- Blueberry Lemon Sorbet 46
- Grape Sorbet 46
- Blueberry & Pomegranate Sorbet 46
- Mojito Sorbet 47
- Mango Margarita Sorbet 47
- Kiwi & Strawberry Sorbet 47
- Mixed Berries Sorbet 47
- Pineapple Sorbet 47

Chapter 7 Milkshake Recipes — 48

- Healthy Strawberry Shake 49
- Chocolate Cherry Milkshake 49
- Lemon Meringue Pie Milkshake 49
- Chocolate-hazelnut Milkshake 49
- Boozy Amaretto Cookie Milkshake 49
- Chocolate–peanut Butter Milkshake 50
- Cacao Mint Milkshake 50
- Amaretto Cookies Milkshake 50
- Frozen Mudslide 50
- Orange Milkshake 50
- Lime Sherbet Milkshake 50
- Chocolate Liqueur Milkshake 51
- Caramel Cone Milkshake 51
- Dairy-free Strawberry Milkshake 51
- Peanut Butter Brownie Milkshake 51
- Vanilla Milkshake 51
- Peanut Butter And Jelly Milkshake 51
- Chocolate Yogurt Milkshake 52
- Sugar Cookie Milkshake 52
- Avocado Milkshake 52
- Marshmallow Milkshake 52
- Cacao Matcha Milkshake 52
- Cashew Butter Milkshake 52
- Pecan Milkshake 53
- Lite Peanut Butter Ice Cream 53
- Dulce De Leche Milkshake 53
- Lite Raspberry Ice Cream 53
- Mixed Berries Milkshake 53
- Chocolate Ice Cream Milkshake 53
- Lite Coffee Chip Ice Cream 54
- Mocha Milkshake 54
- Mocha Tahini Milkshake 54
- Baileys Milkshake 54
- Coffee Vodka Milkshake 54
- Lemon Cookie Milkshake 54
- Banana Milkshake 55
- Chocolate Ginger Milkshake 55
- Chocolate Hazelnut Milkshake 55

INTRODUCTION

I live in a hot place, and because of that, I have a big sweet tooth for cold treats. Ice cream, milkshakes, gelato, and sometimes I go healthy and get myself a smoothie. But there was a problem: everything was becoming too expensive.

Ice cream shops that used to charge a couple of bucks for a two-scoop cone are approaching $10! It's excruciating when I want to take someone out on a date! Not to mention, a lot of products are filled with unhealthy additives.

When I tried to make my own at home, it just wasn't the same. I needed something that was intuitive enough to help me create some amazing recipes, and also didn't break the bank.

The prices of everything was going up too. The sugary products from the stories, from restaurant chains, and the like was becoming a burden. I also didn't like how most of them came with extras, and sometimes, I just wanted to have a sweet treat without the guilt.

Because of that, I had to cut back. I looked for a solution for this problem, since most of it wasn't fitting my budget. But that sweet tooth was too much until I found the Ninja Creami.

This little machine makes everything cold, I love. Ice cream, milkshakes, gelato, smoothies, you name it! It's cheaper to make it at home, and it just tastes better. No more trying to make ice cream with your freezer. Everything tasted much fresher too. I was amazed when I used the recipes, and was able to create the tastiest fruit smoothie I've ever had. Jamba Juice won't even cut it with some of the amazing sweet treats you can make with this!

Because of the Creami, I've become a confectioner. I've been making my ice cream flavors, creating some incredibly healthy and filling smoothies, and creating gelato so good that it saves me money on a trip to Italy. So I am sharing what I created in this handy recipe book.

Don't worry; creating the perfect ice cream is simple with the Creami. Not only that, but my recipes are easy to follow and designed for people of all skill levels.

I also use ingredients you can find at home. Look, I love exotic ice cream now and again, but this cookbook uses recipes you can find at home. And if they're not at your home, you can find them in any convenience store.

So, without further ado, let me show you some of my favorite recipes. You, your friends, and your kids will love many. But before I do so, I want to tell you the basics about the Ninja Creami. It's not the most complicated appliance, but you should know a few simple rules.

Let's begin.

Chapter 1 Ninja Creami Basic Guide

The Ninja Creami is a 7-in-1 cold treat maker designed to help you make homemade ice creams, milkshakes, gelatos, and more. When I purchased the Ninja Creami, I was a little skeptical. How can you make ice cream as good as the local ice cream shop? It seemed so easy to mess it up.

However, the Ninja Creami makes it simple, using easy-to-find ingredients and a quick process to turn them into delicious treats. Let me explain. I will tell you how you can turn your essential ingredients into yummy surprises.

How to Turn Simple Ingredients Into Decadent Treats?

The Ninja Creami works a bit differently from other ice cream makers. Most of them mix in the ingredients, and then you have to freeze it while it's inside the container. However, the Ninja Creami does things backward. Mix some simple ingredients, freeze them overnight, and then put them inside the Creami. Once you do so, it'll mix them into the perfect ice cream.

Because it works in minutes, it's easier to use this to create ice cream. As long as you have some frozen ingredients every day, you can make a fabulous treat each day without much worry.

Later, I'll tell you how to make ice cream specifically, but remember that the initial mixture is not complicated, using ingredients you can find at home. Once you've done this, you can create a frozen delight that your family will love.

Now, let's look at the seven features the Creami has to offer.

Seven One-Touch Programs

The Ninja Creami offers a variety of features. But, first, let's look at all seven of their one-touch programs.

Ice Cream

The classic treat for a hot day or a cold one! You can make delicious ice cream from home, with your imagination only limiting how many flavors you can make. Also, you can make non-dairy ice cream if you're lactose intolerant or vegan. No matter who you are, everyone deserves a nice bowl of ice cream.

Sorbet

Sorbet does not use dairy products or dairy alternatives but instead uses fruit juices to create a healthier option. Sorbet is a little different than ice cream, so this option ensures you get the perfect sorbet every time.

Gelato

In English, gelato refers to a specific type of ice cream of Italian ice cream. Compared to traditional ice cream, gelato is less fattening, denser due to having less air, and focuses on milk instead of cream. Therefore, it has a different texture. Both are good, and it depends on what I'm in the mood for.

Milkshake

This setting lets you make a milkshake with relative ease. With it, you can create the perfect thick, delicious shake with the ingredients perfectly blended in. Great when you want something on-the-go, or even if you want to slurp it up at home. A thick straw is not included.

Smoothie Bowl

Whether you're making yourself a protein smoothie for a workout, a delicious fruit smoothie for a hot day, or a meal replacement smoothie for your health, this feature replaces your separate smoothie maker. The only difference is that you eat it from a bowl rather than drink it. Though, you could put it in a cup, too.

Lite Ice Cream

Trying to watch your weight, but you still love ice cream? This feature lets you make ice cream with less fat. Don't let that fool you, though. It's still simple to create filling, delicious flavors with this option.

+ Mix In

Finally, we have this option, which adds to the six previous options. With it, you can mix fresh ingredients like nuts, berries, Oreos, and so on. The Creami will mix everything to perfection.

Four Outstanding Features

What makes the Ninja Creami pure magic is that it boasts four features that make it appealing to anyone. Let's examine these four features and explain why they are so appealing.

1. Creamify Technology

This describes the magic that lets the Creami make you ice cream in minutes. It does real science stuff, shaving and churning ice cream particles into perfection with ease. I don't have the science degree to describe everything, but it works. We may not have flying cars yet, but we got the next best thing: Creamify Technology.

2. Re-Spin Functionality

This feature lets you make your ice cream even softer and creamier if you aren't satisfied with the first results. We all like different textures of ice cream, and this ensures you get the right flavor for the job. Some people like their ice cream harder, while others like that soft serve. With the Creami, everyone wins.

3. Easy-to-Use

Again, I can't stress how easy it is to make ice cream in this thing. I've tried to make ice cream multiple times in my life, and unfortunately, it never turns out well. I was worried that even Ninja couldn't help me. But I was wrong. This ice cream maker is intuitive and straightforward for anyone, regardless of skill level.

4. Compact-in-Size

The problem with most ice cream makers is that they tend to be significant. Because of this, many who live in smaller apartments with smaller kitchens find that they can't own an ice cream maker. However, the Creami is compact, enabling anyone to make some great ice cream. Even people living in boxes can find enough room to use the Creami and make some delicious frozen treats.

Care and Cleaning

To get the most out of your Creami, clean it after each use. Here's how to do this.

♦ Remove the Creamerizer Paddle from its outer bowl lid. Press the paddle latch after rinsing the lid to remove it.

♦ The container, paddle, and lid are machine-washable on the top rack. Separate each part before putting them in the dishwasher. The dishwasher works best for stuck-on foods, too.

♦ Alternatively, you can hand wash them in soapy, warm water.

♦ To clean the motor base or the exterior of the Creami, you can wipe it down with a damp cloth. Be sure your device is unplugged before you do this.

♦ In addition, read the manual. There, you can learn more tips on cleaning and maintaining your Creami.

And there you have it. Now, let's look at so many recipes. Here's hoping you know how to keep your sweet tooth in check.

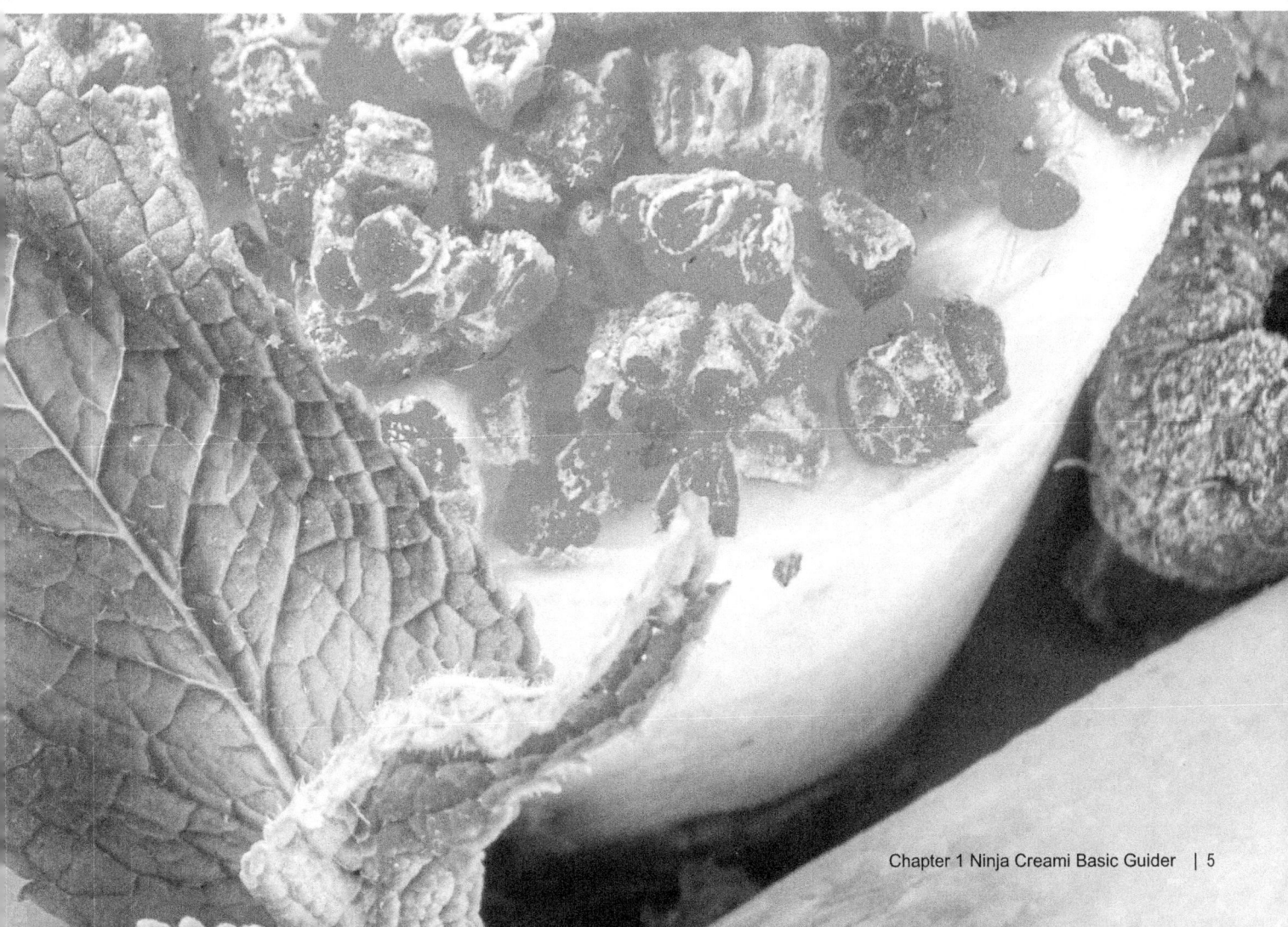

Chapter 2 Ice Cream Mix-ins

Chapter 2 Ice Cream Mix-ins

Chocolate Brownie Ice Cream

Prep time: 5 minutes | Cook time: 3 minutes | Serves 4

- 1 tablespoon cream cheese, softened
- 1/3 cup granulated sugar
- 1 teaspoon vanilla extract
- 2 tablespoons cocoa powder
- 1 cup whole milk
- ¾ cup heavy cream
- 2 tablespoons mini chocolate chips
- 2 tablespoons brownie chunks

1. In a large microwave-safe bowl, add the cream cheese and microwave on High for about ten seconds. 2. Remove from the microwave and stir until smooth. 3. Add the sugar and almond extract and with a wire whisk, beat until the mixture looks like frosting. 4. Slowly add the milk and heavy cream and beat until well combined. 5. Transfer the mixture into an empty Ninja CREAMi pint container. 6. Cover the container with storage lid and freeze for 24 hours. 7. After 24 hours, remove the lid from container and arrange into the Outer Bowl of Ninja CREAMi. 8. Install the Creamerizer Paddle onto the lid of Outer Bowl. 9. Then rotate the lid clockwise to lock. 10. Press Power button to turn on the unit. 11. Then press Ice Cream button. 12. When the program is completed, with a spoon, create a 1½-inch wide hole in the center that reaches the bottom of the pint container. 13. Add the chocolate chunks and brownie pieces into the hole and press Mix-In button. 14. When the program is completed, turn the Outer Bowl and release it from the machine. 15. Transfer the ice cream into serving bowls and serve immediately.

Rocky Road Ice Cream

Prep time: 5 minutes | Cook time: 3 minutes | Serves 4

- 1 cup whole milk
- ½ cup frozen cauliflower florets, thawed
- ½ cup dark brown sugar
- 3 tablespoons dark cocoa powder
- 1 teaspoon chocolate extract
- 1/3 cup heavy cream
- 2 tablespoons almonds, sliced
- 2 tablespoons mini marshmallows
- 2 tablespoons mini chocolate chips

1. In a high-speed blender, add milk, cauliflower, brown sugar, cocoa powder, and chocolate extract and pulse until smooth. 2. Transfer the mixture into an empty Ninja CREAMi pint container. 3. Add the heavy cream and stir until well combined. 4. Cover the container with storage lid and freeze for 24 hours. 5. After 24 hours, remove the lid from container and arrange into the Outer Bowl of Ninja CREAMi. 6. Install the Creamerizer Paddle onto the lid of Outer Bowl. 7. Then rotate the lid clockwise to lock. 8. Press Power button to turn on the unit. 9. Then press Ice Cream button. 10. When the program is completed, with a spoon, create a 1½-inch wide hole in the center that reaches the bottom of the pint container. 11. Add the almonds, marshmallows and chocolate chips into the hole and press Mix-In button. 12. When the program is completed, turn the Outer Bowl and release it from the machine. 13. Transfer the ice cream into serving bowls and serve immediately.

Bourbon-maple-walnut Ice Cream

Prep time: 5 minutes | Cook time: 3 minutes | Serves 4

- 4 large egg yolks
- ¼ cup maple syrup
- ¼ cup corn syrup
- 2 tablespoons bourbon
- ½ cup whole milk
- 1 cup heavy (whipping) cream
- ¼ cup toasted walnut halves

1. Fill a large bowl with ice water and set it aside. 2. In a small saucepan, whisk together the egg yolks, maple syrup, corn syrup, and bourbon until the mixture is fully combined. Do not do this over heat. 3. Whisk in the milk and heavy cream. 4. Place the pan over medium heat. Cook, stirring constantly with a rubber spatula, until the temperature reaches 165°F to 175°F on an instant-read thermometer. 5. Remove the pan from the heat and pour the base into a clean CREAMi Pint. Carefully place the container in the prepared ice water bath, making sure the water doesn't spill into the base. 6. Once the base has cooled, place the storage lid on the pint and freeze for 24 hours. 7. Remove the pint from the freezer and take off the lid. Place the pint in the outer bowl of your Ninja CREAMi, install the Creamerizer Paddle in the outer bowl lid, and lock the lid assembly onto the outer bowl. Place the bowl assembly on the motor base, and twist the handle to the right to raise the platform and lock it in place. Select the Ice Cream function. 8. Once the machine has finished processing, remove the lid from the pint container. With a spoon, create a 1½-inch-wide hole that reaches the bottom of the pint. During this process, it is okay if your treat reaches above the Max Fill line. Add the toasted walnuts to the hole in the pint, replace the lid, and select the Mix-In function. 9. Once the machine has finished processing, remove the ice cream from the pint. Serve immediately.

Pistachio Ice Cream

Prep time: 5 minutes | Cook time: 3 minutes | Serves 4

1 tablespoon cream cheese, softened	1 cup whole milk
⅓ cup granulated sugar	¾ cup heavy cream
1 teaspoon almond extract	¼ cup pistachios, shells removed and chopped

1. In a large microwave-safe bowl, add the cream cheese and microwave on High for about ten seconds. 2. Remove from the microwave and stir until smooth. 3. Add the sugar and almond extract and with a wire whisk, beat until the mixture looks like frosting. 4. Slowly add the milk and heavy cream and beat until well combined. 5. Transfer the mixture into an empty Ninja CREAMi pint container. 6. Cover the container with storage lid and freeze for 24 hours. 7. After 24 hours, remove the lid from container and arrange into the Outer Bowl of Ninja CREAMi. 8. Install the Creamerizer Paddle onto the lid of Outer Bowl. 9. Then rotate the lid clockwise to lock. 10. Press Power button to turn on the unit. 11. Then press Ice Cream button. 12. When the program is completed, with a spoon, create a 1½-inch wide hole in the center that reaches the bottom of the pint container. 13. Add the pistachios into the hole and press Mix-In button. 14. When the program is completed, turn the Outer Bowl and release it from the machine. 15. Transfer the ice cream into serving bowls and serve immediately.

Sneaky Mint Chip Ice Cream

Prep time: 5 minutes | Cook time: 3 minutes | Serves 4

3 large egg yolks	1 cup packed fresh spinach
1 tablespoon corn syrup	½ cup frozen peas, thawed
¼ cup granulated sugar	1 teaspoon mint extract
⅓ cup whole milk	¼ cup semisweet chocolate chips
¾ cup heavy (whipping) cream	

1. Fill a large bowl with ice water and set it aside. 2. In a small saucepan, whisk together the egg yolks, corn syrup, and sugar until the mixture is fully combined and the sugar is dissolved. Do not do this over heat. 3. Whisk in the milk and heavy cream. 4. Place the pan over medium heat. Cook, stirring constantly with a rubber spatula, until the temperature reaches 165°F to 175°F on an instant-read thermometer. 5. Remove the pan from the heat and pour the base into a clean CREAMi Pint. Carefully place the container in the prepared ice water bath, making sure the water doesn't spill into the base. 6. Once the mixture has completely cooled, pour the base into a blender and add the spinach, peas, and mint extract. Blend on high for 30 seconds. Strain the base through a fine-mesh strainer back into the CREAMi Pint. Place the storage lid on the container and freeze for 24 hours. 7. Remove the pint from the freezer and take off the lid. Place the pint in the outer bowl of your Ninja CREAMi, install the Creamerizer Paddle in the outer bowl lid, and lock the lid assembly onto the outer bowl. Place the bowl assembly on the motor base, and twist the handle to the right to raise the platform and lock it in place. Select the Ice Cream function. 8. Once the machine has finished processing, remove the lid from the pint container. With a spoon, create a 1½-inch-wide hole that reaches the bottom of the pint. During this process, it is okay if your treat reaches above the Max Fill line. Add the chocolate chips to the hole in the pint, replace the lid, and select the Mix-In function. 9. Once the machine has finished processing, remove the ice cream from the pint. Serve immediately.

Birthday Cake Ice Cream

Prep time: 5 minutes | Cook time: 3 minutes | Serves 4

5 large egg yolks	1 cup heavy (whipping) cream
¼ cup corn syrup	1½ tablespoons vanilla extract
2½ tablespoons granulated sugar	3 tablespoons vanilla cake mix
⅓ cup whole milk	2 tablespoons rainbow-colored sprinkles

1. Fill a large bowl with ice water and set it aside. 2. In a small saucepan, whisk together the egg yolks, corn syrup, and sugar until the mixture is fully combined and the sugar is dissolved. Do not do this over heat. 3. Whisk in the milk, heavy cream, and vanilla. 4. Place the pan over medium heat. Cook, stirring constantly with a rubber spatula, until the temperature reaches 165°F to 175°F on an instant-read thermometer. 5. Remove the pan from the heat and pour the base through a fine-mesh strainer into a clean CREAMi Pint. Carefully place the container in the prepared ice water bath, making sure the water doesn't spill into the base. 6. Once the base has cooled, whisk in the vanilla cake mix until it is fully incorporated. Place the storage lid on the pint container and freeze for 24 hours. 7. Remove the pint from the freezer and take off the lid. Place the pint in the outer bowl of your Ninja CREAMi, install the Creamerizer Paddle in the outer bowl lid, and lock the lid assembly onto the outer bowl. Place the bowl assembly on the motor base, and twist the handle to the right to raise the platform and lock it in place. Select the Ice Cream function. 8. Once the machine has finished processing, remove the lid from the pint container. With a spoon, create a 1½-inch-wide hole that reaches the bottom of the pint. During this process, it is okay if your treat reaches above the Max Fill line. Add the rainbow sprinkles to the hole in the pint, replace the lid, and select the Mix-In function. 9. Once the machine has finished processing, remove the ice cream from the pint. Serve immediately.

Grasshopper Ice Cream

Prep time: 5 minutes | Cook time: 3 minutes | Serves 4

½ cup frozen spinach, thawed and squeezed dry
1 cup whole milk
½ cup granulated sugar
1 teaspoon mint extract
3-5 drops green food coloring
⅓ cup heavy cream
¼ cup chocolate chunks, chopped
¼ cup brownie, cut into 1-inch pieces

1. In a high-speed blender, add the spinach, milk, sugar, mint extract and food coloring and pulse until mixture smooth. 2. Transfer the mixture into an empty Ninja CREAMi pint container. 3. Add the heavy cream and stir until well combined. 4. Cover the container with storage lid and freeze for 24 hours. 5. After 24 hours, remove the lid from container and arrange into the Outer Bowl of Ninja CREAMi. 6. Install the Creamerizer Paddle onto the lid of Outer Bowl. 7. Then rotate the lid clockwise to lock. 8. Press Power button to turn on the unit. 9. Then press Ice Cream button. 10. When the program is completed, with a spoon, create a 1½-inch wide hole in the center that reaches the bottom of the pint container. 11. Add the chocolate chunks and brownie pieces into the hole and press Mix-In button. 12. When the program is completed, turn the Outer Bowl and release it from the machine. 13. Transfer the ice cream into serving bowls and serve immediately.

Coffee And Cookies Ice Cream

Prep time: 5 minutes | Cook time: 3 minutes | Serves 4

1 tablespoon cream cheese, at room temperature
⅓ cup granulated sugar
1 teaspoon vanilla extract
1 tablespoon instant espresso
¾ cup heavy (whipping) cream
1 cup whole milk
¼ cup crushed chocolate sandwich cookies

1. In a large bowl, whisk together the cream cheese, sugar, and vanilla for about 1 minute, until the mixture looks like frosting. 2. Slowly whisk in the instant espresso, heavy cream, and milk until fully combined. 3. Pour the base into a clean CREAMi Pint. Place the lid on the container and freeze for 24 hours. 4. Remove the pint from the freezer and take off the lid. Place the pint in the outer bowl of your Ninja CREAMi, install the Creamerizer Paddle in the outer bowl lid, and lock the lid assembly onto the outer bowl. Place the bowl assembly on the motor base, and twist the handle to the right to raise the platform and lock it in place. Select the Ice Cream function. 5. Once the machine has finished processing, remove the lid from the pint container. With a spoon, create a 1½-inch-wide hole that reaches the bottom of the pint. Add the crushed cookies to the hole, replace the lid, and select the Mix-In function. 6. Once the machine has finished processing, remove the ice cream from the pint. Serve immediately.

Cookies & Cream Ice Cream

Prep time: 5 minutes | Cook time: 5 minutes | Serves 2

½ tablespoon cream cheese, softened
¼ cup granulated sugar
½ teaspoon vanilla extract
½ cup heavy cream
½ cup whole milk
1½ chocolate sandwich cookies, broken, for mix-in

1. Microwave the cream cheese for 10 seconds in a large microwave-safe bowl. Combine the sugar and vanilla extract in a mixing bowl and whisk or scrape together until the mixture resembles frosting, about 60 seconds. 2. Slowly whisk in the heavy cream and milk until smooth and the sugar has dissolved. 3. Pour the base into an empty CREAMi Pint. Place storage lid on the Pint and freeze for 24 hours. 4. Remove the Pint from the freezer and remove the lid from the Pint. Place the Pint in the outer bowl, install Creamerizer Paddle onto the outer bowl lid, and lock the lid assembly on the outer bowl. Select ICE CREAM. 5. With a spoon, create a 1½-inch wide hole that reaches the bottom of the Pint. During this process, it's okay for your treat to go above the max fill line. Add the broken chocolate sandwich cookies to the hole and process again using the MIX-IN program. 6. When processing is complete, remove the ice cream from the Pint and serve immediately.

Cookies And Coconut Ice Cream

Prep time: 5 minutes | Cook time: 3 minutes | Serves 4

1 can full-fat unsweetened coconut milk
½ cup organic sugar
1 teaspoon vanilla extract
4 chocolate sandwich cookies, crushed

1. In a medium bowl, whisk together the coconut milk, sugar, and vanilla until well combined and the sugar is dissolved. 2. Pour the base into a clean CREAMi Pint. Place the storage lid on the container and freeze for 24 hours. 3. Remove the pint from the freezer and take off the lid. Place the pint in the outer bowl of your Ninja CREAMi, install the Creamerizer Paddle in the outer bowl lid, and lock the lid assembly onto the outer bowl. Place the bowl assembly on the motor base, and twist the handle to the right to raise the platform and lock it in place. Select the Ice Cream function. 4. Once the machine has finished processing, remove the lid from the pint container. With a spoon, create a 1½-inch-wide hole that reaches the bottom of the pint. During this process, it is okay if your treat reaches above the Max Fill line. Add the crushed cookies to the hole in the pint, replace the lid, and select the Mix-In function. 5. Once the machine has finished processing, remove the ice cream from the pint. Serve immediately with desired toppings.

Mint Chocolate Chip Ice Cream

Prep time: 5 minutes | Cook time: 5 minutes | Serves 4

1 tablespoon cream cheese, softened	1 cup whole milk
⅓ cup granulated sugar	1 teaspoon mint extract
1 teaspoon vanilla extract	Green food coloring (optional)
¾ cup heavy cream	¼ cup mini chocolate chips, for mix-in

1. Microwave the cream cheese for 10 seconds in a large microwave-safe bowl. Combine with the sugar and mint extract in a mixing bowl using a whisk or rubber spatula for about 60 seconds or until the mixture resembles frosting. 2. Slowly whisk in the heavy cream, milk, and optional food coloring until thoroughly mixed and the sugar has dissolved. 3. Pour the base into an empty CREAMi Pint. Place the storage lid on the Pint and freeze for 24 hours. 4. Remove the Pint from the freezer and remove its lid. Place the Pint in the outer bowl, install the Creamerizer Paddle onto the outer bowl lid, and lock the lid assembly on the outer bowl. Place the bowl assembly on the motor base, twist the handle to raise the platform, and lock it in place. 5. Select ICE CREAM. 6. With a spoon, create a 1½-inch wide hole that reaches the bottom of the Pint. During this process, it's okay for your treat to press above the max fill line. Add the chocolate chips to the hole and process again using the MIX-IN program.

Coffee Chip Ice Cream

Prep time: 5 minutes | Cook time: 3 minutes | Serves 4

¾ cup heavy cream	1 cup unsweetened almond milk
¼ cup monk fruit sweetener with Erythritol	1 teaspoon vanilla extract
½ teaspoon stevia sweetener	3 tablespoons chocolate chips
1½ tablespoons instant coffee granules	1 tablespoon walnuts, chopped

1. In a bowl, add the heavy cream and beat until smooth. 2. Add the remaining ingredients except for chocolate chips and walnuts and beat sweetener is dissolved. 3. Transfer the mixture into an empty Ninja CREAMi pint container. 4. Cover the container with storage lid and freeze for 24 hours. 5. After 24 hours, remove the lid from container and arrange into the Outer Bowl of Ninja CREAMi. 6. Install the Creamerizer Paddle onto the lid of Outer Bowl. 7. Then rotate the lid clockwise to lock. 8. Press Power button to turn on the unit. 9. Then press Lite Ice Cream button. 10. When the program is completed, with a spoon, create a 1½-inch wide hole in the center that reaches the bottom of the pint container. 11. Add the chocolate chips and walnuts into the hole and press Mix-In button. 12. When the program is completed, turn the Outer Bowl and release it from the machine. 13. Transfer the ice cream into serving bowls and serve immediately.

Mint Cookies Ice Cream

Prep time: 5 minutes | Cook time: 3 minutes | Serves 4

¾ cup coconut cream	5-6 drops green food coloring
¼ cup monk fruit sweetener with Erythritol	1 cup oat milk
2 tablespoons agave nectar	3 chocolate sandwich cookies, quartered
½ teaspoon mint extract	

1. In a large bowl, add the coconut cream and beat until smooth. 2. Add the sweetener, agave nectar, mint extract and food coloring and beat until sweetener is dissolved. 3. Add the oat milk and beat until well combined. 4. Transfer the mixture into an empty Ninja CREAMi pint container. 5. Cover the container with storage lid and freeze for 24 hours. 6. After 24 hours, remove the lid from container and arrange into the Outer Bowl of Ninja CREAMi. 7. Install the Creamerizer Paddle onto the lid of Outer Bowl. 8. Then rotate the lid clockwise to lock. 9. Press Power button to turn on the unit. 10. Then press Lite Ice Cream button. 11. When the program is completed, with a spoon, create a 1½-inch wide hole in the center that reaches the bottom of the pint container. 12. Add the cookie pieces into the hole and press Mix-In button. 13. When the program is completed, turn the Outer Bowl and release it from the machine. 14. Transfer the ice cream into serving bowls and serve immediately.

Sweet Potato Pie Ice Cream

Prep time: 5 minutes | Cook time: 3 minutes | Serves 4

1 cup canned pureed sweet potato	1 teaspoon vanilla extract
1 tablespoon corn syrup	1 teaspoon cinnamon
¼ cup plus 1 tablespoon light brown sugar	¾ cup heavy (whipping) cream
	¼ cup mini marshmallows

1. Combine the sweet potato puree, corn syrup, brown sugar, vanilla, and cinnamon in a blender. Blend on high until smooth. 2. Pour the base into a clean CREAMi Pint. Whisk in the heavy cream until combined. Place the storage lid on the container and freeze for 24 hours. 3. Remove the pint from the freezer and take off the lid. Place the pint in the outer bowl of your Ninja CREAMi, install the Creamerizer Paddle in the outer bowl lid, and lock the lid assembly onto the outer bowl. Place the bowl assembly on the motor base, and twist the handle to the right to raise the platform and lock it in place. Select the Ice Cream function. 4. Once the machine has finished processing, remove the lid from the pint container. With a spoon, create a 1½-inch-wide hole that reaches the bottom of the pint. During this process, it is okay if your treat reaches above the Max Fill line. Add the marshmallows to the hole in the pint, replace the lid, and select the Mix-In function. 5. Once the machine has finished processing, remove the ice cream from the pint. Serve immediately with desired toppings.

Vanilla Ice Cream With Chocolate Chips

Prep time: 5 minutes | Cook time: 5 minutes | Serves 4

1 tablespoon cream cheese, softened
⅓ cup granulated sugar
1 teaspoon vanilla extract
¾ cup heavy cream
1 cup whole milk
¼ cup mini chocolate chips, for mix-in

1. Microwave the cream cheese for 10 seconds in a large microwave-safe bowl. With a rubber spatula, blend in the sugar and vanilla extract until the mixture resembles frosting, about 60 seconds. 2. Slowly whisk in the heavy cream and milk until smooth and the sugar has dissolved. 3. Pour the base into an empty CREAMi Pint. Place the storage lid on the Pint and freeze for 24 hours. 4. Remove the Pint from the freezer and remove the lid from the Pint. Place the Pint in the outer bowl, install the Creamerizer Paddle onto the outer bowl lid, and lock the lid assembly on the outer bowl. Select ICE CREAM. 5. With a spoon, create a 1½-inch wide hole that reaches the bottom of the Pint. During this process, it's okay for your treat to press above the max fill line. Add chocolate chips to the hole in the Pint and process again using the MIX-IN program. 6. When processing is complete, remove the ice cream from the Pint.

Coconut Mint Chip Ice Cream

Prep time: 5 minutes | Cook time: 3 minutes | Serves 4

1 can full-fat unsweetened coconut milk
½ cup organic sugar
½ teaspoon mint extract
¼ cup mini vegan chocolate chips

1. In a medium bowl, whisk together the coconut milk, sugar, and mint extract until everything is well combined and the sugar is dissolved. 2. Pour the base into a clean CREAMi Pint. Place the storage lid on the container and freeze for 24 hours. 3. Remove the pint from the freezer and take off the lid. Place the pint in the outer bowl of your Ninja CREAMi, install the Creamerizer Paddle in the outer bowl lid, and lock the lid assembly onto the outer bowl. Place the bowl assembly on the motor base, and twist the handle to the right to raise the platform and lock it in place. Select the Ice Cream function. 4. Once the machine has finished processing, remove the lid from the pint container. With a spoon, create a 1½-inch-wide hole that reaches the bottom of the pint. During this process, it is okay if your treat reaches above the Max Fill line. Add the mini chocolate chips to the hole in the pint, replace the lid, and select the Mix-In function. 5. Once the machine has finished processing, remove the ice cream from the pint. Serve immediately with desired toppings.

Lavender Cookie Ice Cream

Prep time: 5 minutes | Cook time: 10 minutes | Serves 4

¾ cup heavy cream
1 tablespoon dried culinary lavender
⅛ teaspoon salt
¾ cup whole milk
½ cup sweetened condensed milk
4 drops purple food coloring
⅓ cup chocolate wafer cookies, crushed

1. In a medium saucepan, add heavy cream, lavender and salt and mix well. 2. Place the saucepan over low heat and steep, covered for about ten minutes, stirring after every two minutes. 3. Remove from the heat and through a fine-mesh strainer, strain the cream mixture into a large bowl. 4. Discard the lavender leaves. 5. In the bowl of cream mixture, add the milk, condensed milk and purple food coloring and beat until smooth. 6. Transfer the mixture into an empty Ninja CREAMi pint container. 7. Cover the container with storage lid and freeze for 24 hours. 8. After 24 hours, remove the lid from container and arrange into the Outer Bowl of Ninja CREAMi. 9. Install the Creamerizer Paddle onto the lid of Outer Bowl. 10. Then rotate the lid clockwise to lock. 11. Press Power button to turn on the unit. 12. Then press Ice Cream button. 13. When the program is completed, with a spoon, create a 1½-inch wide hole in the center that reaches the bottom of the pint container. 14. Add the crushed cookies the hole and press Mix-In button. 15. When the program is completed, turn the Outer Bowl and release it from the machine. 16. Transfer the ice cream into serving bowls and serve immediately.

Jelly & Peanut Butter Ice Cream

Prep time: 5 minutes | Cook time: 5 minutes | Serves 4

3 tablespoons granulated sugar
4 large egg yolks
1 cup whole milk
⅓ cup heavy cream
¼ cup smooth peanut butter
3 tablespoons grape jelly
¼ cup honey roasted peanuts, chopped

1. In a small saucepan, add the sugar and egg yolks and beat until sugar is dissolved. 2. Add the milk, heavy cream, peanut butter, and grape jelly to the saucepan and stir to combine. 3. Place saucepan over medium heat and cook until temperature reaches cook until temperature reaches to 165 -175° F, stirring continuously with a rubber spatula. 4. Remove from the heat and through a fine-mesh strainer, strain the mixture into an empty Ninja CREAMi pint container. 5. Place the container into ice bath to cool. 6. After cooling, cover the container with storage lid and freeze for 24 hours. 7. After 24 hours, remove the lid from container and arrange into the Outer Bowl of Ninja CREAMi. 8. Install the Creamerizer Paddle onto the lid of Outer Bowl. 9. Then rotate the lid clockwise to lock. 10. Press Power button to turn on the unit. 11. Then press ICE CREAM button. 12. When the program is completed, with a spoon, create a 1½-inch wide hole in the center that reaches the bottom of the pint container. 13. Add the peanuts into the hole and press Mix-In button. 14. When the program is completed, turn the Outer Bowl and release it from the machine. 15. Transfer the ice cream into serving bowls and serve immediately.

Triple-chocolate Ice Cream

Prep time: 5 minutes | Cook time: 3 minutes | Serves 4

4 large egg yolks	¾ cup heavy (whipping) cream
⅓ cup granulated sugar	½ cup whole milk
1 tablespoon unsweetened cocoa powder	1 teaspoon vanilla extract
	¼ cup white chocolate chips
1 tablespoon hot fudge sauce	

1. Fill a large bowl with ice water and set it aside. 2. In a small saucepan, whisk together the egg yolks, sugar, and cocoa powder until the mixture is fully combined and the sugar is dissolved. Do not do this over heat. 3. Whisk in the hot fudge, heavy cream, milk, and vanilla. 4. Place the pan over medium heat. Cook, stirring constantly with a rubber spatula, until the temperature reaches 165°F to 175°F on an instant-read thermometer. 5. Remove the pan from the heat and pour the base through a fine-mesh strainer into a clean CREAMi Pint. Carefully place the container in the prepared ice water bath, making sure the water doesn't spill into the base. 6. Once the base has cooled, place the storage lid on the pint and freeze for 24 hours. 7. Remove the pint from the freezer and take off the lid. Place the pint in the outer bowl of your Ninja CREAMi, install the Creamerizer Paddle in the outer bowl lid, and lock the lid assembly onto the outer bowl. Place the bowl assembly on the motor base, and twist the handle to the right to raise the platform and lock it in place. Select the Ice Cream function. 8. Once the machine has finished processing, remove the lid from the pint container. With a spoon, create a 1½-inch-wide hole that reaches the bottom of the pint. During this process, it is okay if your treat reaches above the Max Fill line. Add the white chocolate chips to the hole in the pint, replace the lid, and select the Mix-In function. 9. Once the machine has finished processing, remove the ice cream from the pint. Serve immediately with desired toppings.

Fruity Cereal Ice Cream

Prep time: 5 minutes | Cook time: 30 minutes | Serves 2

¾ cup whole milk	¼ cup granulated sugar
1 cup fruity cereal, divided	1 teaspoon vanilla extract
1 tablespoon Philadelphia cream cheese, softened	½ cup heavy cream

1. In a large mixing bowl, combine ½ cup of the fruity cereal and the milk. Allow the mixture to settle for 15–30 minutes, stirring occasionally to infuse the milk with the fruity taste. 2. Microwave the Philadelphia cream cheese for 10 seconds in a second large microwave-safe dish. Combine the sugar and vanilla extract in a mixing bowl with a whisk or rubber spatula until the mixture resembles frosting, about 60 seconds. 3. After 15 to 30 minutes, sift the milk and cereal into the bowl with the sugar mixture using a fine-mesh filter. To release extra milk, press on the cereal with a spoon, then discard it. Mix in the heavy cream until everything is thoroughly mixed. 4. Pour the mixture into an empty ninja CREAMi Pint container. Add the strawberries to the Pint, making sure not to go over the max fill line, and freeze for 24 hours. 5. After 24 hours, remove the Pint from the freezer. Remove the lid. 6. Place the Ninja CREAMi Pint into the outer bowl. Place the outer bowl with the Pint in it into the ninja CREAMi machine and turn until the outer bowl locks into place. Push the ICE CREAM button. During the ICE CREAM function, the ice cream will mix together and become very creamy. 7. Use a spoon to create a 1½-inch wide hole that reaches the bottom of the Pint. Add the remaining ½ cup of fruity cereal to the hole and process again using the mix-in. When processing is complete, remove the ice cream from the Pint.

Lite Chocolate Cookie Ice Cream

Prep time: 5 minutes | Cook time: 5 minutes | Serves 2

1 tablespoon cream cheese, at room temperature	1 teaspoon vanilla extract
	¾ cup heavy cream
2 tablespoons unsweetened cocoa powder	1 cup whole milk
	¼ cup crushed reduced-fat sugar cookies
½ teaspoon stevia sweetener	
3 tablespoons raw agave nectar	

1. Place the cream cheese in a large microwave-safe bowl and heat on high for 10 seconds. 2. Mix in the cocoa powder, stevia, agave, and vanilla. Microwave for 60 seconds more, or until the mixture resembles frosting. 3. Slowly whisk in the heavy cream and milk until the sugar has dissolved and the mixture is thoroughly mixed. 4. Pour the base into a clean CREAMi Pint. Place the storage lid on the container and freeze for 24 hours. 5. Remove the Pint from the freezer and take off the lid. Place the Pint in the outer bowl of your Ninja CREAMi, install the Creamerizer Paddle in the outer bowl lid, and lock the lid assembly onto the outer bowl. Place the bowl assembly on the motor base, and twist the handle to the right to raise the platform and lock it in place. Select the LITE ICE CREAM function. 6. Once the machine has finished processing, remove the lid. With a spoon, create a 1½-inch-wide hole that reaches the bottom of the Pint. During this process, it's okay if your treat goes above the max fill line. Add the crushed cookies to the hole in the Pint. Replace the Pint lid and select the MIX-IN function. 7. Once the machine has finished processing, remove the ice cream from the Pint.

Rum Raisin Ice Cream

Prep time: 5 minutes | Cook time: 23 minutes | Serves 4

- 3 large egg yolks
- ¼ cup dark brown sugar (or coconut sugar)
- 1 tablespoon light corn syrup
- ½ cup heavy cream
- 1 cup whole milk
- 1 teaspoon rum extract
- ⅓ cup raisins
- ¼ cup dark or spiced rum

1. In a small saucepan, combine the egg yolks, sugar, and corn syrup. Whisk until everything is well mixed and the sugar has dissolved. Whisk together the heavy cream and milk until smooth. 2. Stir the mixture frequently with a whisk or a rubber spatula in a saucepan over medium-low heat. Using an instant-read thermometer, cook until the temperature hits 165°F–175°F. 3. Remove the base from heat, stir in the rum extract, then pour through a fine-mesh strainer into an empty CREAMi Pint. Place into an ice bath. Once cooled, place the storage lid on the Pint and freeze for 24 hours. 4. While the base is cooling, prepare the mix-in. Add the raisins and rum to a small bowl and microwave for 1 minute. Let cool, then drain the remaining rum. Cover and set aside. 5. Remove the Pint from the freezer and remove its lid. Place the Pint in the outer bowl, install the Creamerizer Paddle onto the outer bowl lid, and lock the lid assembly on the outer bowl. Select ICE CREAM. 6. With a spoon, create a 1½-inch wide hole that reaches the bottom of the Pint. Add the mixed raisins to the hole and process again using the MIX-IN program. 7. When processing is complete, remove the ice cream from the Pint.

Snack Mix Ice Cream

Prep time: 5 minutes | Cook time: 10 seconds | Serves 4

- 1 tablespoon cream cheese, softened
- ⅓ cup granulated sugar
- ½ teaspoon vanilla extract
- 1 cup whole milk
- ¾ cup heavy cream
- 2 tablespoons sugar cone pieces
- 1 tablespoon mini pretzels
- 1 tablespoon potato chips, crushed

1. In a large microwave-safe bowl, add the cream cheese and microwave on High for about ten seconds. 2. Remove from the microwave and stir until smooth. 3. Add the sugar and vanilla extract and with a wire whisk, beat until the mixture looks like frosting. 4. Slowly add the milk and heavy cream and beat until well combined. 5. Transfer the mixture into an empty Ninja CREAMi pint container. 6. Cover the container with storage lid and freeze for 24 hours. 7. After 24 hours, remove the lid from container and arrange into the Outer Bowl of Ninja CREAMi. 8. Install the Creamerizer Paddle onto the lid of Outer Bowl. 9. Then rotate the lid clockwise to lock. 10. Press Power button to turn on the unit. 11. Then press Ice Cream button. 12. When the program is completed, with a spoon, create a 1½-inch wide hole in the center that reaches the bottom of the pint container. 13. Add the cone pieces, pretzels and potato chips into the hole and press Mix-In button. 14. When the program is completed, turn the Outer Bowl and release it from the machine. 15. Transfer the ice cream into serving bowls and serve immediately.

Lavender Cookies & Cream Ice Cream

Prep time: 8 minutes | Cook time: 20 minutes | Serves 2

- ½ cup heavy cream
- ½ tablespoon dried culinary lavender
- ¼ teaspoon kosher salt
- ½ cup whole milk
- ¼ cup sweetened condensed milk
- 2 drops purple food coloring
- ¼ cup crushed chocolate wafer cookies

1. Whisk together the heavy cream, lavender, and salt in a medium saucepan. 2. Steep the mixture for 10 minutes over low heat, stirring every 2 minutes to prevent bubbling. 3. Using a fine-mesh strainer, drain the lavender from the heavy cream into a large mixing basin. Discard the lavender. 4. Combine the milk, sweetened condensed milk, and purple food coloring in a large mixing bowl. Whisk until the mixture is completely smooth. 5. Pour the base into an empty CREAMi Pint. Place the Pint into an ice bath. Once cooled, place the storage lid on the Pint and freeze for 24 hours. 6. Remove the Pint from the freezer and remove its lid. Place Pint in outer bowl, install Creamerizer Paddle in outer bowl lid, and lock the lid assembly onto the outer bowl. Select ICE CREAM. 7. When the process is done, create a 1½-inch wide hole that reaches the bottom of the Pint with a spoon. It's okay if your treat exceeds the max fill line. Add crushed wafer cookies to the hole and process again using the MIX-IN program. 8. When processing is complete, remove ice cream from Pint and serve immediately, topped with extra crumbled wafers if desired.

Chapter 3 Ice Cream Recipes

Chapter 3 Ice Cream Recipes

Carrot Ice Cream

Prep time: 5 minutes | Cook time: 1 minutes | Serves 2

1 cup heavy cream
½ cup carrot juice
⅓ cup light brown sugar
2 tablespoons cream cheese frosting
1 teaspoon vanilla extract
1 teaspoon ground cinnamon

1. In a bowl, add all ingredients and beat until well combined. 2. Transfer the mixture into an empty Ninja CREAMi pint container. 3. Cover the container with the storage lid and freeze for 24 hours 4. After 24 hours, remove the lid from container and arrange into the outer bowl of Ninja CREAMi. 5. Install the "Creamerizer Paddle" onto the lid of outer bowl. 6. Then rotate the lid clockwise to lock. 7. Press "Power" button to turn on the unit. 8. Then press "ICE CREAM" button. 9. When the program is completed, turn the outer bowl and release it from the machine. 10. Transfer the ice cream into serving bowls and serve immediately.

Classic Vanilla Ice Cream

Prep time: 5 minutes | Cook time: 5 minutes | Serves 4

1 tablespoon cream cheese, at room temperature
⅓ cup granulated sugar
1 teaspoon vanilla extract
¾ cup heavy (whipping) cream
1 cup whole milk
¼ cup mini chocolate chips (optional)

1. In a large microwave-safe bowl, add the cream cheese and microwave for 10 seconds. Add the sugar and vanilla extract, and with a whisk or rubber spatula, combine the mixture until it looks like frosting, about 60 seconds. 2. Slowly whisk in the heavy cream and milk and mix until the sugar is completely dissolved and the cream cheese is completely incorporated. 3. Pour the base into a clean CREAMi Pint. Place the storage lid on the container and freeze for 24 hours. 4. Remove the CREAMi Pint from the freezer and take off the lid. Place the pint container in the outer bowl of your Ninja CREAMi, install the Creamerizer Paddle in the outer bowl lid, and lock the lid assembly onto the outer bowl. Place the bowl assembly on the motor base, and twist the handle to the right to raise the platform and lock it in place. Select the Ice Cream function. 5. Once the machine has finished processing, remove the lid from the pint container. If you are adding chocolate chips: with a spoon, create a 1½-inch-wide hole that reaches the bottom of the pint. During this process, it is okay if your treat reaches above the Max Fill line. Add ¼ cup of mini chocolate chips to the hole in the pint, replace the lid, and select the Mix-In function. 6. Serve immediately with desired toppings.

Peanut Butter Ice Cream

Prep time: 5 minutes | Cook time: 5 minutes | Serves 4

1¾ cups skim milk
3 tablespoons smooth peanut butter
¼ cup stevia-cane sugar blend
1 teaspoon vanilla extract

1. In a bowl, add all ingredients and beat until smooth. 2. Set aside for about five minutes. 3. Transfer the mixture into an empty Ninja CREAMi pint container. 4. Cover the container with storage lid and freeze for 24 hours. 5. After 24 hours, remove the lid from container and arrange into the outer bowl of Ninja CREAMi. 6. Install the Creamerizer Paddle onto the lid of Outer Bowl. 7. Then rotate the lid clockwise to lock. 8. Press Power button to turn on the unit. 9. Then press Ice Cream button. 10. When the program is completed, turn the Outer Bowl and release it from the machine. 11. Transfer the ice cream into serving bowls and serve immediately.

Coffee Ice Cream

Prep time: 5 minutes | Cook time: 5 minutes | Serves 4

¾ cup coconut cream
½ cup granulated sugar
1½ tablespoons instant coffee
powder
1 cup rice milk
1 teaspoon vanilla extract

1. In a bowl, add coconut cream and beat until smooth. 2. Add the remaining ingredients and beat sugar is dissolved. 3. Transfer the mixture into an empty Ninja CREAMi pint container. 4. Cover the container with storage lid and freeze for 24 hours. 5. After 24 hours, remove the lid from container and arrange into the Outer Bowl of Ninja CREAMi. 6. Install the Creamerizer Paddle onto the lid of Outer Bowl. 7. Then rotate the lid clockwise to lock. 8. Press Power button to turn on the unit. 9. Then press Ice Cream button. 10. When the program is completed, turn the Outer Bowl and release it from the machine. 11. Transfer the ice cream into serving bowls and serve immediately.

Matcha Ice Cream

Prep time: 5 minutes | Cook time: 10 seconds | Serves 4

1 tablespoon cream cheese, softened
⅓ cup granulated sugar
2 tablespoons matcha powder
1 teaspoon vanilla extract
1 cup whole milk
¾ cup heavy cream

1. In a large microwave-safe bowl, add the cream cheese and microwave for on High for about ten seconds. 2. Remove from the microwave and stir until smooth. 3. Add the sugar, matcha powder and vanilla extract and with a wire whisk, beat until the mixture looks like frosting. 4. Slowly add the milk and heavy cream and beat until well combined. 5. Transfer the mixture into an empty Ninja CREAMi pint container. 6. Cover the container with storage lid and freeze for 24 hours. 7. After 24 hours, remove the lid from container and arrange into the Outer Bowl of Ninja CREAMi. 8. Install the Creamerizer Paddle onto the lid of Outer Bowl. 9. Then rotate the lid clockwise to lock. 10. Press Power button to turn on the unit. 11. Then press Ice Cream button. 12. When the program is completed, turn the Outer Bowl and release it from the machine. 13. Transfer the ice cream into serving bowls and serve immediately.

Earl Grey Tea Ice Cream

Prep time: 5 minutes | Cook time: 25 minutes | Serves 4

1 cup heavy cream
1 cup whole milk
5 tablespoons monk fruit
sweetener
3 Earl Grey tea bags

1. In a medium saucepan, add cream and milk and stir to combine. 2. Place saucepan over medium heat and cook until for bout two-three minutes or until steam is rising. 3. Stir in the monk fruit sweetener and reduce the heat to very low. 4. Add teabags and cover the saucepan for about 20 minutes. 5. Discard the tea bags and remove saucepan from heat. 6. Transfer the mixture into an empty Ninja CREAMi pint container and place into an ice bath to cool. 7. After cooling, cover the container with storage lid and freeze for 24 hours. 8. After 24 hours, remove the lid from container and arrange into the Outer Bowl of Ninja CREAMi. 9. Install the Creamerizer Paddle onto the lid of Outer Bowl. 10. Then rotate the lid clockwise to lock. 11. Press Power button to turn on the unit. 12. Then press Ice Cream button. 13. When the program is completed, turn the Outer Bowl and release it from the machine. 14. Transfer the ice cream into serving bowls and serve immediately.

Sea Salt Caramel Ice Cream

Prep time: 5 minutes | Cook time: 5 minutes | Serves 4

4 large egg yolks
1 tablespoon dark brown sugar
3 tablespoons prepared caramel sauce
⅓ cup whole milk
1 cup heavy (whipping) cream
1 teaspoon sea salt

1. Fill a large bowl with ice water and set it aside. 2. In a small saucepan, whisk the egg yolks, brown sugar, and caramel sauce until the mixture is fully combined and the sugar is dissolved. Do not do this over heat. 3. Whisk in the milk, heavy cream, and sea salt until combined. 4. Place the pan over medium heat. Using a rubber spatula, stir constantly and cook until the temperature reaches 165°F to 175°F on an instant-read thermometer. 5. Remove the pan from the heat and pour the base through a fine-mesh strainer into a CREAMi Pint. Carefully place the pint in the prepared ice water bath, making sure the water doesn't spill into the base. 6. Once the base has cooled, place the storage lid on the pint container and freeze for 24 hours. 7. Remove the CREAMi Pint from the freezer and take off the lid. Place the pint in the outer bowl of your Ninja CREAMi, install the Creamerizer Paddle in the outer bowl lid, and lock the lid assembly onto the outer bowl. Place the bowl assembly on the motor base, and twist the handle to the right to raise the platform and lock it in place. Select the Ice Cream function. 8. Once the machine has finished processing, remove the ice cream from the pint. Serve immediately with desired toppings.

Peanut Butter & Jelly Ice Cream

Prep time: 5 minutes | Cook time: 5 minutes | Serves 4

3 tablespoons granulated sugar
4 large egg yolks
1 cup whole milk
⅓ cup heavy cream
¼ cup smooth peanut butter
3 tablespoons grape jelly
¼ cup honey roasted peanuts, chopped

1. In a small saucepan, add the sugar and egg yolks and beat until well combined. 2. Add the milk, heavy cream, peanut butter, and grape jelly to the saucepan and stir to combine. 3. Place saucepan over medium heat and for about 3-5 minutes, stirring continuously. 4. Remove from the heat and through a fine-mesh strainer, strain the mixture into an empty Ninja CREAMi pint container. 5. Place the container into an ice bath to cool. 6. After cooling, cover the container with the storage lid and freeze for 24 hours. 7. After 24 hours, remove the lid from container and arrange into the outer bowl of Ninja CREAMi. 8. Install the "Creamerizer Paddle" onto the lid of outer bowl. 9. Then rotate the lid clockwise to lock. 10. Press "Power" button to turn on the unit. 11. Then press "ICE CREAM" button. 12. When the program is completed, with a spoon, create a 1½-inch wide hole in the center that reaches the bottom of the pint container. 13. Add the peanuts into the hole and press "MIX-IN" button. 14. When the program is completed, turn the outer bowl and release it from the machine. 15. Transfer the ice cream into serving bowls and serve immediately.

Strawberry Ice Cream

Prep time: 5 minutes | Cook time: 5 minutes | Serves 4

¼ cup sugar
1 tablespoon cream cheese, softened
1 teaspoon vanilla bean paste
1 cup milk
¾ cup heavy whipping cream
6 medium fresh strawberries, hulled and quartered

1. In a bowl, add the sugar, cream cheese, vanilla bean paste and with a wire whisk, mix until well combined. 2. Add in the milk and heavy whipping cream and beat until well combined. 3. Transfer the mixture into an empty Ninja CREAMi pint container. 4. Add the strawberry pieces and stir to combine. 5. Cover the container with storage lid and freeze for 24 hours. 6. After 24 hours, remove the lid from container and arrange into the Outer Bowl of Ninja CREAMi. 7. Install the Creamerizer Paddle onto the lid of Outer Bowl. 8. Then rotate the lid clockwise to lock. 9. Press Power button to turn on the unit. 10. Then press Ice Cream button. 11. When the program is completed, turn the Outer Bowl and release it from the machine. 12. Transfer the ice cream into serving bowls and serve immediately.

Mocha Ice Cream

Prep time: 5 minutes | Cook time: 5 minutes | Serves 4

½ cup mocha cappuccino mix
1¾ cups coconut cream
3 tablespoons agave nectar

1. In a bowl, add all ingredients and beat until well combined. 2. Transfer the mixture into an empty Ninja CREAMi pint container. 3. Cover the container with storage lid and freeze for 24 hours. 4. After 24 hours, remove the lid from container and arrange into the Outer Bowl of Ninja CREAMi. 5. Install the Creamerizer Paddle onto the lid of Outer Bowl. 6. Then rotate the lid clockwise to lock. 7. Press Power button to turn on the unit. 8. Then press Ice Cream button. 9. When the program is completed, turn the Outer Bowl and release it from the machine. 10. Transfer the ice cream into serving bowls and serve immediately.

Pear Ice Cream

Prep time: 5 minutes | Cook time: 15 minutes | Serves 4

3 medium ripe pears, peeled, cored and cut into 1-inch pieces
1 can full-fat unsweetened coconut milk
½ cup granulated sugar

1. In a medium saucepan, add all ingredients and stir to combine. 2. Place the saucepan over medium heat and bring to a boil. 3. Reduce the heat to low and simmer for about ten minutes or until liquid is reduced by half. 4. Remove from the heat and set aside to cool. 5. After cooling, transfer the mixture into a high-speed blender and pulse until smooth. 6. Transfer the mixture into an empty Ninja CREAMi pint container. 7. Cover the container with storage lid and freeze for 24 hours. 8. After 24 hours, remove the lid from container and arrange into the Outer Bowl of Ninja CREAMi. 9. Install the Creamerizer Paddle onto the lid of Outer Bowl. 10. Then rotate the lid clockwise to lock. 11. Press Power button to turn on the unit. 12. Then press Ice Cream button. 13. When the program is completed, turn the Outer Bowl and release it from the machine. 14. Transfer the ice cream into serving bowls and serve immediately.

Fruity Carrot Ice Cream

Prep time: 5 minutes | Cook time: 5 minutes | Serves 4

¾ cup heavy cream
½ cup milk
⅓ cup orange juice
¾ cup sugar
¼ cup frozen carrots
¼ cup pineapple chunks

1. In a bowl, add the heavy cream, milk, orange juice and sugar and beat until well combined. 2. In an empty Ninja CREAMi pint container, place the carrots and pineapple chunks and top with milk mixture. 3. Cover the container with the storage lid and freeze for 24 hours. 4. After 24 hours, remove the lid from container and arrange into the outer bowl of Ninja CREAMi. 5. Install the "Creamerizer Paddle" onto the lid of outer bowl. 6. Then rotate the lid clockwise to lock. 7. Press "Power" button to turn on the unit. 8. Then press "ICE CREAM" button. 9. When the program is completed, turn the outer bowl and release it from the machine. 10. Transfer the ice cream into serving bowls and serve immediately.

Low-sugar Vanilla Ice Cream

Prep time: 5 minutes | Cook time: 5 minutes | Serves 4

1¾ cup fat-free half-and-half
¼ cup stevia cane sugar blend
1 teaspoon vanilla extract

1. In a medium bowl, whisk the half-and-half, sugar, and vanilla together until everything is combined and the sugar is dissolved. The mixture will be foamy. Let it sit for 5 minutes or until the foam subsides. 2. Pour the base into a clean CREAMi Pint. Place the storage lid on the container and freeze for 24 hours. 3. Remove the CREAMi Pint from the freezer and take off the lid. Place the pint in the outer bowl of your Ninja CREAMi, install the Creamerizer Paddle in the outer bowl lid, and lock the lid assembly onto the outer bowl. Place the bowl assembly on the motor base, and twist the handle to the right to raise the platform and lock it in place. Select the Lite Ice Cream function. 4. Once the machine has finished processing, remove the ice cream from the pint. Serve immediately.

Coconut-vanilla Ice Cream

Prep time: 5 minutes | Cook time: 5 minutes | Serves 4

1 can full-fat unsweetened coconut milk	½ cup organic sugar
	1 teaspoon vanilla extract

1. In a large bowl, whisk together the coconut milk, sugar, and vanilla until everything is incorporated and the sugar is dissolved. 2. Pour the base into a clean CREAMi Pint. Place the storage lid on the container and freeze for 24 hours. 3. Remove the CREAMi Pint from the freezer and take off the lid. Place the pint in the outer bowl of your Ninja CREAMi, install the Creamerizer Paddle in the outer bowl lid, and lock the lid assembly onto the outer bowl. Place the bowl assembly on the motor base, and twist the handle to the right to raise the platform and lock it in place. Select the Ice Cream function. 4. Once the machine has finished processing, remove the ice cream from the pint. Serve immediately with desired toppings.

Strawberry-carrot Ice Cream

Prep time: 5 minutes | Cook time: 5 minutes | Serves 4

1 cup frozen carrot slices, thawed	⅓ cup granulated sugar
½ cup trimmed and quartered fresh strawberries	1 teaspoon strawberry extract
	½ cup whole milk
	5 drops red food coloring
1 tablespoon cream cheese, at room temperature	½ cup heavy (whipping) cream

1. Combine the carrots, strawberries, cream cheese, sugar, strawberry extract, milk, and food coloring in a blender. Blend on high until smooth. 2. Pour the base into a clean CREAMi Pint. Whisk in the heavy cream until combined. Place the storage lid on the container and freeze for 24 hours. 3. Remove the CREAMi Pint from the freezer and take off the lid. Place the pint in the outer bowl of your Ninja CREAMi, install the Creamerizer Paddle in the outer bowl lid, and lock the lid assembly onto the outer bowl. Place the bowl assembly on the motor base, and twist the handle to the right to raise the platform and lock it in place. Select the Ice Cream function. 4. Once the machine has finished processing, remove the ice cream from the pint. Serve immediately with desired toppings.

Coconut Ice Cream

Prep time: 5 minutes | Cook time: 5 minutes | Serves 4

½ cup milk	¾ cup heavy cream
1 can cream of coconut	½ cup sweetened flaked coconut

1. In a food processor or blender, combine the milk and coconut cream and thoroughly mix. 2. Combine the heavy cream and flaked coconut in a mixing bowl, and then add to the milk-cream mixture. Combine well. 3. Pour the mixture into an empty ninja CREAMi Pint container and freeze for 24 hours. 4. After 24 hours, remove the Pint from the freezer. Remove the lid. 5. Place the Ninja CREAMi Pint into the outer bowl. Place the outer bowl with the Pint in it into the ninja CREAMi machine and turn until the outer bowl locks into place. Push the ICE CREAM button. 6. Once the ICE CREAM function has ended, turn the outer bowl and release it from the ninja CREAMi machine.

Blueberry Ice Cream

Prep time: 5 minutes | Cook time: 5 minutes | Serves 4

1 cup blueberries	¼ cup milk
½ cup vanilla whole milk Greek yogurt	2 tablespoons honey
	2 tablespoons chia seeds

1. In a bowl, add all ingredients and eat until well combined. 2. Transfer the mixture into an empty Ninja CREAMi pint container. 3. Cover the container with storage lid and freeze for 24 hours. 4. After 24 hours, remove the lid from container and arrange into the Outer Bowl of Ninja CREAMi. 5. Install the Creamerizer Paddle onto the lid of Outer Bowl. 6. Then rotate the lid clockwise to lock. 7. Press Power button to turn on the unit. 8. Then press Ice Cream button. 9. When the program is completed, turn the Outer Bowl and release it from the machine. 10. Transfer the ice cream into serving bowls and serve immediately.

Creamy Caramel Macchiato Coffee Ice Cream

Prep time: 5 minutes | Cook time: 5 minutes | Serves 6

1 cup heavy whipping cream	(liquid creamer)
½ cup sweetened condensed milk	1 teaspoon instant coffee granules
¼ cup coffee-mate caramel macchiato flavored creamer	Caramel syrup (for drizzling)

1. Combine all ingredients (except the syrup) in a big mixing bowl of a stand mixer or a large mixing dish. 2. Whip the heavy cream mixture with an electric mixer until firm peaks form (to prevent massive splattering, start at a slower speed, and as the cream thickens, increase the speed). Make sure the whip cream mixture isn't overmixed or "broken." 3. Pour the mixture into an empty ninja CREAMi Pint container and freeze for 24 hours. 4. After 24 hours, remove the Pint from the freezer. Remove the lid. 5. Place the Ninja CREAMi Pint into the outer bowl. Place the outer bowl with the Pint in it into the ninja CREAMi machine and turn until the outer bowl locks into place. Push the ICE CREAM button. 6. Once the ICE CREAM function has ended, turn the outer bowl and release it from the ninja CREAMi machine.

Kale'd By Chocolate Ice Cream

Prep time: 5 minutes | Cook time: 5 minutes | Serves 4

1 cup frozen kale	3 tablespoons dark unsweetened cocoa powder
1 tablespoon cream cheese, at room temperature	¾ cup whole milk
⅓ cup granulated sugar	¾ cup heavy (whipping) cream

1. Combine the frozen kale, cream cheese, sugar, cocoa powder, and milk in a blender. Blend on high until smooth. 2. Pour the base into a clean CREAMi Pint. Whisk in the heavy cream until combined. Place the storage lid on the container and freeze for 24 hours. 3. Remove the CREAMi Pint from the freezer and take off the lid. Place the pint in the outer bowl of your Ninja CREAMi, install the Creamerizer Paddle in outer bowl lid, and lock the lid assembly onto the outer bowl. Place the bowl assembly on the motor base, and twist the handle to the right to raise the platform and lock it in place. Select the Ice Cream function. 4. Once the machine has finished processing, remove the ice cream from the pint. Serve immediately with desired toppings.

French Vanilla Ice Cream

Prep time: 5 minutes | Cook time: 5 minutes | Serves 4

4 large egg yolks	⅓ cup whole milk
1 tablespoon light corn syrup	1 cup heavy (whipping) cream
¼ cup plus 1 tablespoon granulated sugar	1 teaspoon vanilla extract

1. Fill a large bowl with ice water and set it aside. 2. In a small saucepan, whisk together the egg yolks, corn syrup, and sugar until the mixture is fully combined and the sugar is dissolved. Do not do this over heat. 3. Whisk in the milk, heavy cream, and vanilla until combined. 4. Place the pan over medium heat. Cook, stirring constantly with a rubber spatula, until the temperature reaches 165°F to 175°F on an instant-read thermometer. 5. Remove the pan from the heat and pour the base through a fine-mesh strainer into a clean CREAMi Pint. Carefully place the container in the prepared ice water bath, making sure the water doesn't spill into the base. 6. Once the base has cooled, place the storage lid on the pint and freeze for 24 hours. 7. Remove the CREAMi Pint from the freezer and take off the lid. Place the pint in the outer bowl of your Ninja CREAMi, install the Creamerizer Paddle in the outer bowl lid, and lock the lid assembly onto the outer bowl. Place the bowl assembly on the motor base, and twist the handle to the right to raise the platform and lock it in place. Select the Ice Cream function. 8. Once the machine has finished processing, remove the ice cream from the pint. Serve immediately.

Super Lemon Ice Cream

Prep time: 5 minutes | Cook time: 20 minutes | Serves 5

1 cup heavy whipping cream	1 tablespoon grated lemon zest
½ cup half-and-half cream	2 egg yolks
½ cup white sugar	¼ cup fresh lemon juice

1. On low heat, whisk together the heavy cream, half-and-half cream, sugar, and lemon zest in a saucepan until the sugar is dissolved. 2. In a mixing dish, whisk together the egg yolks. 3. Stir in a few tablespoons of the cream mixture at a time into the eggs. This will assist in bringing the eggs up to temperature without them becoming scrambled. Return the egg mixture to the bowl with the cream mixture. 4. Pour the mixture into an empty ninja CREAMi Pint container, add lemon, and freeze for 24 hours. 5. After 24 hours, remove the Pint from the freezer. Remove the lid. 6. Place the Ninja CREAMi Pint into the outer bowl. Place the outer bowl with the Pint in it into the ninja CREAMi machine and turn until the outer bowl locks into place. Push the ICE CREAM button. 7. Once the ICE CREAM function has ended, turn the outer bowl and release it from the ninja CREAMi machine.

Mint Cookie Ice Cream

Prep time: 5 minutes | Cook time: 5 minutes | Serves 4

¾ cup coconut cream	5-6 drops green food coloring
¼ cup monk fruit sweetener with Erythritol	1 cup oat milk
2 tablespoons agave nectar	3 chocolate sandwich cookies, quartered
½ teaspoon mint extract	

1. In a large bowl, add the coconut cream and beat until smooth. 2. Add the sweetener, agave nectar, mint extract and food coloring and beat until sweetener is dissolved. 3. Add the oat milk and beat until well combined. 4. Transfer the mixture into an empty Ninja CREAMi pint container. 5. Cover the container with the storage lid and freeze for 24 hours. 6. After 24 hours, remove the lid from container and arrange into the outer bowl of Ninja CREAMi. 7. Install the "Creamerizer Paddle" onto the lid of outer bowl. 8. Then rotate the lid clockwise to lock. 9. Press "Power" button to turn on the unit. 10. Then press "LITE ICE CREAM" button. 11. When the program is completed, with a spoon, create a 1½-inch wide hole in the center that reaches the bottom of the pint container. 12. Add the cookie pieces into the hole and press "MIX-IN" button. 13. When the program is completed, turn the outer bowl and release it from the machine. 14. Transfer the ice cream into serving bowls and serve immediately.

Chocolate Ice Cream

Prep time: 5 minutes | Cook time: 5 minutes | Serves 1

¾ cup heavy whipping cream	½ cup unsweetened cocoa powder
½ can sweetened condensed milk	½ teaspoon vanilla extract

1. In a medium mixing bowl, combine the sweetened condensed milk, cocoa powder, and vanilla extract. 2. In a separate bowl, whip the heavy cream until it forms firm peaks (do not overbeat). 3. Pour mixture into an empty ninja CREAMi Pint container and freeze for 24 hours. 4. After 24 hours, remove the Pint from the freezer. Remove the lid. 5. Place the Ninja CREAMi Pint into the outer bowl. Place the outer bowl with the Pint in it into the ninja CREAMi machine and turn until the outer bowl locks into place. Push the ICE CREAM button. During the ICE CREAM function, the ice cream will mix together and become very creamy. 6. Once the ICE CREAM function has ended, turn the outer bowl and release it from the ninja CREAMi machine.

Cinnamon Red Hot Ice Cream

Prep time: 5 minutes | Cook time: 10 minutes | Serves 5

2 cups heavy whipping cream, divided	1 cup half-and-half
1 egg yolk	½ cup Red Hot candies

1. In a mixing bowl, whisk together 1 cup of cream and the egg yolks until smooth. 2. In another large bowl, combine the half-and-half, 1 cup cream, and Red Hot candies. Whisk with a wooden spoon until the candies dissolve, about 5 to 10 minutes. 3. Pour the cream-egg mixture into the candy mixture and stir to incorporate. 4. Pour the mixture into an empty ninja CREAMi Pint container and freeze for 24 hours. 5. After 24 hours, remove the Pint from the freezer. Remove the lid. 6. Place the Ninja CREAMi Pint into the outer bowl. Place the outer bowl with the Pint in it into the ninja CREAMi machine and turn until the outer bowl locks into place. Push the ICE CREAM button. 7. Once the ICE CREAM function has ended, turn the outer bowl and release it from the ninja CREAMi machine.

Blackberry Ice Cream

Prep time: 5 minutes | Cook time: 5 minutes | Serves 2

½ pint fresh blackberries	1 cup heavy cream
¼ cup white sugar	⅓ cup whole milk
½ teaspoon lemon zest	1 teaspoon vanilla extract

1. Puree the blackberries, sugar, and lemon zest in a blender. 2. Put the purée in a mixing bowl after straining the seeds through a fine-mesh sieve. 3. Combine the cream, milk, and vanilla extract in a mixing bowl. Mix for about 30 seconds or until the mixture is whipped. Add to the purée and mix well. 4. Pour the mixture into an empty ninja CREAMi Pint container and freeze for 24 hours. 5. After 24 hours, remove the Pint from the freezer. Remove the lid. 6. Place the Ninja CREAMi Pint into the outer bowl. Place the outer bowl with the Pint in it into the ninja CREAMi machine and turn until the outer bowl locks into place. Push the ICE CREAM button. 7. Once the ICE CREAM function has ended, turn the outer bowl and release it from the ninja CREAMi machine.

Mango Ice Cream

Prep time: 5 minutes | Cook time: 5 minutes | Serves 1

1 mango (medium-sized, cut into quarters)	¼ cup sugar
1 tablespoon cream cheese (room temperature)	¾ cup heavy whipping cream
	1 cup milk

1. Combine the cream cheese, sugar in a mixing bowl. Using a whisk, mix together until all ingredients are thoroughly combined, and the sugar starts to dissolve. 2. Add in the heavy whipping cream and milk. Whisk until all ingredients have combined well. 3. Pour mixture into an empty ninja CREAMi Pint container. Freeze for 24 hours after adding the mango to the Pint, ensuring you don't go over the maximum fill line. 4. Take the Pint out of the freezer after 24 hours. Take off the cover. 5. Place the Ninja CREAMi Pint into the outer bowl. Place the outer bowl with the Pint in it into the ninja CREAMi machine and turn until the outer bowl locks into place. Push the ICE CREAM button. During the ICE CREAM function, the ice cream will mix and become very creamy. 11. Once the ICE CREAM function has ended, turn the outer bowl and release it from the ninja CREAMi machine.

Lemon Ice Cream

Prep time: 5 minutes | Cook time: 5 minutes | Serves 4

1 can full-fat unsweetened coconut milk	1 teaspoon vanilla extract
½ cup granulated sugar	1 teaspoon lemon extract

1. In a bowl, add the coconut milk and beat until smooth. 2. Add the remaining ingredients and beat until sugar is dissolved. 3. Transfer the mixture into an empty Ninja CREAMi pint container. 4. Cover the container with storage lid and freeze for 24 hours. 5. After 24 hours, remove the lid from container and arrange into the Outer Bowl of Ninja CREAMi. 6. Install the Creamerizer Paddle onto the lid of Outer Bowl. 7. Then rotate the lid clockwise to lock. 8. Press Power button to turn on the unit. 9. Then press Ice Cream button. 10. When the program is completed, turn the Outer Bowl and release it from the machine. 11. Transfer the ice cream into serving bowls and serve immediately.

Cherry-chocolate Chunk Ice Cream

Prep time: 5 minutes | Cook time: 10 minutes | Serves 4

1 packet frozen sweet cherries
¾ cup heavy cream
1 can sweetened condensed milk
½ cup milk
1 teaspoon vanilla extract
1 bar semisweet baking chocolate, broken into small chunks

1. Combine the heavy cream, sweetened condensed milk, milk, and vanilla extract in a mixing bowl. 2. Pour the ice cream mixture into an empty ninja CREAMi Pint container, add the chopped cherries and chocolate chunks, and freeze for 24 hours. 3. After 24 hours, remove the Pint from the freezer. Remove the lid. 4. Place the Ninja CREAMi Pint into the outer bowl. Place the outer bowl with the Pint in it into the ninja CREAMi machine and turn until the outer bowl locks into place. Push the ICE CREAM button. 5. Once the ICE CREAM function has ended, turn the outer bowl and release it from the ninja CREAMi machine.

Chocolate & Spinach Ice Cream

Prep time: 5 minutes | Cook time: 5 minutes | Serves 2

½ cup frozen spinach, thawed and squeezed dry
1 cup whole milk
½ cup granulated sugar
1 teaspoon mint extract
3-5 drops green food coloring
⅓ cup heavy cream
¼ cup chocolate chunks, chopped
¼ cup brownie, cut into 1-inch pieces

1. In a high-speed blender, add the spinach, milk, sugar, mint extract and food coloring and pulse until mixture smooth. 2. Transfer the mixture into an empty Ninja CREAMi pint container. 3. Add the heavy cream and stir until well combined. 4. Cover the container with the storage lid and freeze for 24 hours. 5. After 24 hours, remove the lid from container and arrange into the outer bowl of Ninja CREAMi. 6. Install the "Creamerizer Paddle" onto the lid of outer bowl 7. Then rotate the lid clockwise to lock. 8. Press "Power" button to turn on the unit. 9. Then press "ICE CREAM" button. 10. When the program is completed, with a spoon, create a 1½-inch wide hole in the center that reaches the bottom of the pint container. 11. Add the chocolate chunks and brownie pieces into the hole and press "MIX-IN" button. 12. When the program is completed, turn the outer bowl and release it from the machine. 13. Transfer the ice cream into serving bowls and serve immediately.

Philadelphia-style Chocolate Ice Cream

Prep time: 5 minutes | Cook time: 5 minutes | Serves 4

1 tablespoon cream cheese, at room temperature
1 tablespoon unsweetened cocoa powder
⅓ cup granulated sugar
1 teaspoon vanilla extract
¾ cup heavy (whipping) cream
1 cup whole milk

1. In a large microwave-safe bowl, add the cream cheese and microwave for 10 seconds. Add the cocoa powder, sugar, and vanilla extract, and with a whisk or rubber spatula, combine the mixture until it looks like frosting, about 60 seconds. 2. Slowly mix in the heavy cream and milk until everything is fully combined and the sugar is dissolved. 3. Pour the base into a clean CREAMi Pint. Place the storage lid on the container and freeze for 24 hours. 4. Remove the CREAMi Pint from the freezer and take off the lid. Place the pint in the outer bowl of your Ninja CREAMi, install the Creamerizer Paddle in the outer bowl lid, and lock the lid assembly onto the outer bowl. Place the bowl assembly on the motor base, and twist the handle to the right to raise the platform and lock it in place. Select the Ice Cream function. 5. Once the machine has finished processing, remove the ice cream from the pint. Serve immediately with desired toppings.

Fruity Extract Ice Cream

Prep time: 5 minutes | Cook time: 5 minutes | Serves 4

1 cup whole milk
¾ cup heavy cream
2 tablespoons monk fruit sweetener with Erythritol
2 tablespoons agave nectar
½ teaspoon raspberry extract
½ teaspoon vanilla extract
¼ teaspoon lemon extract
5-6 drops blue food coloring

1. In a bowl, add all ingredients and eat until well combined. 2. Transfer the mixture into an empty Ninja CREAMi pint container. 3. Cover the container with storage lid and freeze for 24 hours. 4. After 24 hours, remove the lid from container and arrange into the Outer Bowl of Ninja CREAMi. 5. Install the Creamerizer Paddle onto the lid of outer bowl. 6. Then rotate the lid clockwise to lock. 7. Press Power button to turn on the unit. 8. Then press Ice Cream button. 9. When the program is completed, turn the Outer Bowl and release it from the machine. 10. Transfer the ice cream into serving bowls and serve immediately.

Pumpkin Gingersnap Ice Cream

Prep time: 5 minutes | Cook time: 15 minutes | Serves 4

1 cup heavy whipping cream
½ tablespoon vanilla extract
½ teaspoon ground cinnamon
½ teaspoon ground ginger

½ cup solid-pack pumpkin
1 can Eagle Brand sweetened condensed milk
½ cup crushed gingersnap cookies

1. In a large mixing bowl, beat the heavy whipping cream, vanilla extract, cinnamon, and ginger with an electric mixer on medium speed until stiff peaks form. 2. Combine the pumpkin and sweetened condensed milk in a mixing bowl. 3. Add the crushed gingersnap cookies to the pumpkin mixture and stir well. 4. Pour the mixture into an empty ninja CREAMi Pint container and freeze for 24 hours. 5. After 24 hours, remove the Pint from the freezer. Remove the lid. 6. Place the Ninja CREAMi Pint into the outer bowl. Place the outer bowl with the Pint in it into the ninja CREAMi machine and turn until the outer bowl locks into place. Push the ICE CREAM button. 7. Once the ICE CREAM function has ended, turn the outer bowl and release it from the ninja CREAMi machine.

Chapter 4 Gelato Recipes

Chapter 4 Gelato Recipes

Cherry Gelato

Prep time: 6 minutes | Cook time: 3 minutes | Serves 4

4 large egg yolks
1 tablespoon light corn syrup
5 tablespoons granulated sugar
1 cup heavy cream
⅓ cup whole milk
1 teaspoon almond extract
1 cup frozen black cherries, pitted and quartered

1. In a small saucepan, add the egg yolks, sugar and corn syrup and beat until well combined. 2. Add the heavy cream, milk and almond extract and beat until well combined. 3. Place the saucepan over medium heat and cook for about 2-3 minutes, stirring continuously. 4. Remove from the heat and through a fine-mesh strainer, strain the mixture into an empty Ninja CREAMi pint container. 5. Place the container into an ice bath to cool. 6. After cooling, cover the container with the storage lid and freeze for 24 hours. 7. After 24 hours, remove the lid from container and arrange into the outer bowl of Ninja CREAMi. 8. Install the "Creamerizer Paddle" onto the lid of outer bowl. 9. Then rotate the lid clockwise to lock. 10. Press "Power" button to turn on the unit. 11. Then press "GELATO" button. 12. When the program is completed, with a spoon, create a 1½-inch wide hole in the center that reaches the bottom of the pint container. 13. Add the cherries into the hole and press "MIX-IN" button. 14. When the program is completed, turn the outer bowl and release it from the machine. 15. Transfer the gelato into serving bowls and serve immediately.

Cantaloupe Sorbet

Prep time: 5 minutes | Cook time: 10 minutes | Serves 4

3 cups cantaloupe pieces
⅓ cup water
⅓ cup organic sugar
1 tablespoon freshly squeezed lemon juice

1. Combine the cantaloupe, water, sugar, and lemon juice in a blender. Blend on high until smooth. 2. Pour the base into a clean CREAMi Pint. Place the storage lid on the container and freeze for 24 hours. 3. Remove the pint from the freezer and take off the lid. Place the pint in the outer bowl of your Ninja CREAMi, install the Creamerizer Paddle in the outer bowl lid, and lock the lid assembly onto the outer bowl. Place the bowl assembly on the motor base, and twist the handle to the right to raise the platform and lock it in place. Select the Sorbet function. 4. Once the machine has finished processing, remove the sorbet from the pint. Serve immediately.

Orange Sherbet

Prep time: 5 minutes | Cook time: 3 minutes | Serves 4

1 cup orange juice
¼ cup plus 1 tablespoon granulated sugar
¼ cup whole milk
½ cup heavy (whipping) cream

1. In a large bowl, whisk together the orange juice, sugar, milk, and heavy cream until everything is well combined and the sugar is dissolved. 2. Pour the base into a clean CREAMi Pint. Place the storage lid on the container and freeze for 24 hours. 3. Remove the pint from the freezer and take off the lid. Place the pint in the outer bowl of your Ninja CREAMi, install the Creamerizer Paddle in the outer bowl lid, and lock the lid assembly onto the outer bowl. Place the bowl assembly on the motor base, and twist the handle to the right to raise the platform and lock it in place. Select the Ice Cream function. 4. Once the machine has finished processing, remove the sherbet from the pint. Serve immediately with desired toppings.

Triple Chocolate Gelato

Prep time: 5 minutes | Cook time: 3 minutes | Serves 4

4 large egg yolks
⅓ cup dark brown sugar
2 tablespoons dark cocoa powder
1 tablespoon chocolate fudge topping
¾ cup heavy cream
¾ cup whole milk
2-3 tablespoons chocolate chunks, chopped

1. In a small saucepan, add the egg yolks, sugar, cocoa powder and chocolate fudge and beat until well combined. 2. Add the heavy cream and milk and beat until well combined. 3. Place the saucepan over medium heat and cook for about 2-3 minutes, stirring continuously. 4. Remove from the heat and stir in chocolate chunks until melted completely. 5. Through a fine-mesh strainer, strain the mixture into an empty Ninja CREAMi pint container. 6. Place the container into an ice bath to cool. 7. After cooling, cover the container with the storage lid and freeze for 24 hours. 8. After 24 hours, remove the lid from container and arrange into the outer bowl of Ninja CREAMi. 9. Install the "Creamerizer Paddle" onto the lid of outer bowl. 10. Then rotate the lid clockwise to lock. 11. Press "Power" button to turn on the unit. 12. Then press "GELATO" button. 13. When the program is completed, turn the outer bowl and release it from the machine. 14. Transfer the gelato into serving bowls and serve immediately.

Banana & Squash Cookie Gelato

Prep time: 5 minutes | Cook time: 3 minutes | Serves 4

4 large egg yolks	chopped
1 cup heavy cream	1 box instant vanilla pudding mix
⅓ cup granulated sugar	
½ of banana, peeled and sliced	6 vanilla wafer cookies, crumbled
½ cup frozen butternut squash,	

1. In a small saucepan, add the egg yolks, heavy cream and sugar and beat until well combined. 2. Place the saucepan over medium heat and cook for about 2-3 minutes, stirring continuously. 3. Remove from the heat and through a fine-mesh strainer, strain the mixture into an empty Ninja CREAMi pint container. 4. Place the container into an ice bath to cool. 5. After cooling, add in the banana, squash and pudding until well combined. 6. Cover the container with the storage lid and freeze for 24 hours. 7. After 24 hours, remove the lid from container and arrange into the outer bowl of Ninja CREAMi. 8. Install the "Creamerizer Paddle" onto the lid of outer bowl. 9. Then rotate the lid clockwise to lock. 10. Press "Power" button to turn on the unit. 11. Then press "GELATO" button. 12. When the program is completed, with a spoon, create a 1½-inch wide hole in the center that reaches the bottom of the pint container. 13. Add the wafer cookies into the hole and press "MIX-IN" button. 14. When the program is completed, turn the outer bowl and release it from the machine. 15. Transfer the gelato into serving bowls and serve immediately.

Vanilla Gelato

Prep time: 5 minutes | Cook time: 3 minutes | Serves 4

4 large egg yolks	1 cup heavy cream
1 tablespoon light corn syrup	⅓ cup whole milk
¼ cup plus 1 tablespoon granulated sugar	1 whole vanilla bean, split in half lengthwise and scraped

1. In a small saucepan, add the egg yolks, corn syrup and sugar and beat until well combined. 2. Add the heavy cream, milk and vanilla bean and beat until well combined. 3. Place the saucepan over medium heat and cook for about 2-3 minutes, stirring continuously. 4. Remove from the heat and through a fine-mesh strainer, strain the mixture into an empty Ninja CREAMi pint container. 5. Place the container into an ice bath to cool. 6. After cooling, cover the container with the storage lid and freeze for 24 hours. 7. After 24 hours, remove the lid from container and arrange into the outer bowl of Ninja CREAMi. 8. Install the "Creamerizer Paddle" onto the lid of outer bowl. 9. Then rotate the lid clockwise to lock. 10. Press "Power" button to turn on the unit. 11. Then press "GELATO" button. 12. When the program is completed, turn the outer bowl and release it from the machine. 13. Transfer the gelato into serving bowls and serve immediately.

Chocolate Cauliflower Gelato

Prep time: 15 minutes | Cook time: 3 minutes | Serves 4

1 cup whole milk	½ cup frozen cauliflower rice
½ cup heavy cream	¼ teaspoon almond extract
⅓ cup sugar	Pinch of salt
2 tablespoons cocoa powder	½ cup dark chocolate, chopped

1. In a small saucepan, add all ingredients except for chopped chocolate and beat until well combined. 2. Place the saucepan over medium heat and cook for about 2-3 minutes, stirring continuously. 3. Remove from the heat and transfer the mixture into an empty Ninja CREAMi pint container. 4. Place the container into an ice bath to cool. 5. After cooling, cover the container with the storage lid and freeze for 24 hours. 6. After 24 hours, remove the lid from container and arrange into the outer bowl of Ninja CREAMi. 7. Install the "Creamerizer Paddle" onto the lid of outer bowl. 8. Then rotate the lid clockwise to lock. 9. Press "Power" button to turn on the unit. 10. Then press "GELATO" button. 11. When the program is completed, with a spoon, create a 1½-inch wide hole in the center that reaches the bottom of the pint container. 12. Add the chopped chocolate into the hole and press "MIX-IN" button. 13. When the program is completed, turn the outer bowl and release it from the machine. 14. Transfer the gelato into serving bowls and serve immediately.

Chocolate Hazelnut Gelato

Prep time: 5 minutes | Cook time: 3 minutes | Serves 4

3 large egg yolks	1 tablespoon light corn syrup
⅓ cup hazelnut spread	1 cup whole milk
¼ cup granulated sugar	½ cup heavy cream
2 teaspoons cocoa powder	1 teaspoon vanilla extract

1. In a small saucepan, add the egg yolks, hazelnut spread, sugar, cocoa powder and corn syrup and beat until well combined. 2. Add the milk, heavy cream and vanilla extract and beat until well combined. 3. Place the saucepan over medium heat and cook for about 2-3 minutes, stirring continuously. 4. Remove from the heat and through a fine-mesh strainer, strain the mixture into an empty Ninja CREAMi pint container. 5. Place the container into an ice bath to cool. 6. After cooling, cover the container with the storage lid and freeze for 24 hours. 7. After 24 hours, remove the lid from container and arrange into the outer bowl of Ninja CREAMi. 8. Install the "Creamerizer Paddle" onto the lid of outer bowl. 9. Then rotate the lid clockwise to lock. 10. Press "Power" button to turn on the unit. 11. Then press "GELATO" button. 12. When the program is completed, turn the outer bowl and release it from the machine. 13. Transfer the gelato into serving bowls and serve immediately.

Maple Gelato

Prep time: 5 minutes | Cook time: 3 minutes | Serves 4

4 large egg yolks	1 teaspoon maple extract
½ cup plus 1 tablespoon light brown sugar	1 cup whole milk
	⅓ cup heavy cream
1 tablespoon maple syrup	

1. In a small saucepan, add the egg yolks, brown sugar, maple syrup and maple extract and beat until well combined. 2. Add the milk and heavy cream and beat until well combined. 3. Place the saucepan over medium heat and cook for about 2-3 minutes, stirring continuously. 4. Remove from the heat and through a fine-mesh strainer, strain the mixture into an empty Ninja CREAMi pint container. 5. Place the container into an ice bath to cool. 6. After cooling, cover the container with the storage lid and freeze for 24 hours. 7. After 24 hours, remove the lid from container and arrange into the outer bowl of Ninja CREAMi. 8. Install the "Creamerizer Paddle" onto the lid of outer bowl. 9. Then rotate the lid clockwise to lock. 10. Press "Power" button to turn on the unit. 11. Then press "GELATO" button. 12. When the program is completed, turn the outer bowl and release it from the machine. Transfer the gelato into serving bowls and serve immediately.

Marshmallow Cookie Gelato

Prep time: 5 minutes | Cook time: 6 minutes | Serves 4

1 whole vanilla bean, split in half lengthwise, scraped	1 tablespoon light corn syrup
4 egg yolks	1 teaspoon vanilla extract
¾ cup heavy cream	5 tablespoons marshmallow paste
⅓ cup whole milk	5 peanut butter cookies, chopped
2 tablespoons granulated sugar	

1. In a medium saucepan, add the vanilla bean over medium-high heat, and toast for about 2-3 minutes, stirring continuously. 2. Reduce the heat to medium-low and whisk in the egg yolks, heavy cream, milk, sugar, corn syrup and vanilla extract. 3. Cook for about 2-3 minutes, stirring continuously. 4. Remove from the heat and through a fine-mesh strainer, strain the mixture into an empty Ninja CREAMi pint container. 5. Place the container into an ice bath to cool. 6. After cooling, cover the container with the storage lid and freeze for 24 hours. 7. After 24 hours, remove the lid from container and arrange into the outer bowl of Ninja CREAMi. 8. Install the "Creamerizer Paddle" onto the lid of outer bowl. 9. Then rotate the lid clockwise to lock. 10. Press "Power" button to turn on the unit. 11. Then press "GELATO" button. 12. When the program is completed, with a spoon, create a 1½-inch wide hole in the center that reaches the bottom of the pint container. 13. Add the cookies into the hole and press "MIX-IN" button. 14. When the program is completed, turn the outer bowl and release it from the machine. 15. Transfer the gelato into serving bowls and serve immediately.

Apple Cider Sorbet

Prep time: 5 minutes | Cook time: 3 minutes | Serves 4

1 cup apple cider	2 tablespoons organic sugar
1 cup applesauce	

1. In a large bowl, whisk together the apple cider, applesauce, and sugar until the sugar is dissolved. 2. Pour the base into a clean CREAMi Pint. Place the storage lid on the container and freeze for 24 hours. 3. Remove the pint from the freezer and take off the lid. Place the pint in the outer bowl of your Ninja CREAMi, install the Creamerizer Paddle in the outer bowl lid, and lock the lid assembly onto the outer bowl. Place the bowl assembly on the motor base, and twist the handle to the right to raise the platform and lock it in place. Select the Sorbet function. 4. Once the machine has finished processing, remove the sorbet from the pint. Serve immediately.

Berries Mascarpone Gelato

Prep time: 5 minutes | Cook time: 3 minutes | Serves 4

3 large egg yolks	¾ cup whole milk
½ cup plus 2 tablespoons granulated sugar, divided	¼ cup heavy cream
	½ teaspoon vanilla extract
1 tablespoon light corn syrup	1 cup frozen mixed berries
½ cup mascarpone	

1. In a small saucepan, add the egg yolks, ½ cup of sugar and corn syrup and beat until well combined. 2. Add the mascarpone milk, heavy cream and vanilla extract and beat until well combined. 3. Place the saucepan over medium heat and cook for about 2-3 minutes, stirring continuously. 4. Remove from the heat and through a fine-mesh strainer, strain the mixture into an empty Ninja CREAMi pint container. 5. Place the container into an ice bath to cool. 6. After cooling, cover the container with the storage lid and freeze for 24 hours. 7. Meanwhile, in a small saucepan, add the mixed berries and remaining sugar over medium heat and cook for about 8 minutes, stirring occasionally and mashing to form a thick jam. 8. Remove from heat and transfer the jam into a bowl. 9. Refrigerate the jam until using. 10. After 24 hours, remove the lid from container and arrange the container into the outer bowl of Ninja CREAMi. 11. Install the "Creamerizer Paddle" onto the lid of outer bowl. 12. Then rotate the lid clockwise to lock. 13. Press "Power" button to turn on the unit. 14. Then press "GELATO" button. 15. When the program is completed, with a spoon, create a 1½-inch wide hole in the center that reaches the bottom of the pint container. 16. Add the berry jam into the hole and press "MIX-IN" button. 17. When the program is completed, turn the outer bowl and release it from the machine. 18. Transfer the gelato into serving bowls and serve immediately.

Sweet Potato Gelato

Prep time: 5 minutes | Cook time: 3 minutes | Serves 4

½ cup canned sweet potato puree
4 large egg yolks
¼ cup sugar
½ teaspoon ground cinnamon
⅛ teaspoon ground nutmeg
1 cup heavy cream
1 teaspoon vanilla extract

1. In a small saucepan, add the sweet potato puree, egg yolks, sugar, ½ teaspoon of cinnamon and nutmeg and beat until well combined. 2. Add the heavy cream and vanilla extract and beat until well combined. 3. Place the saucepan over medium heat and cook for about 2-3 minutes, stirring continuously. 4. Remove from the heat and through a fine-mesh strainer, strain the mixture into an empty Ninja CREAMi pint container. 5. Place the container into an ice bath to cool. 6. After cooling, cover the container with the storage lid and freeze for 24 hours. 7. After 24 hours, remove the lid from container and arrange into the outer bowl of Ninja CREAMi. 8. Install the "Creamerizer Paddle" onto the lid of outer bowl. 9. Then rotate the lid clockwise to lock. 10. Press "Power" button to turn on the unit. 11. Then press "GELATO" button. 12. When the program is completed, turn the outer bowl and release it from the machine. 13. Transfer the gelato into serving bowls and serve immediately.

Peanut Butter Gelato

Prep time: 20 minutes | Cook time: 10 minutes | Serves 4

1½ Cups unsweetened coconut milk
6 tablespoons sugar
1 tablespoon cornstarch
3 tablespoons peanut butter
3 dark chocolate peanut butter Cups, cut each into 8 pieces
2 tablespoons peanuts, chopped

1. In a small saucepan, add the coconut milk, sugar, and cornstarch and mix well. 2. Place the saucepan over medium heat and bring to a boil, beating continuously. 3. Reduce the heat to low and simmer for about 3-4 minutes. 4. Remove from the heat and stir in the peanut butter. 5. Transfer the mixture into an empty Ninja CREAMi pint container. 6. Place the container into an ice bath to cool. 7. After cooling, cover the container with the storage lid and freeze for 24 hours. 8. After 24 hours, remove the lid from container and arrange into the outer bowl of Ninja CREAMi. 9. Install the "Creamerizer Paddle" onto the lid of outer bowl. 10. Then rotate the lid clockwise to lock. 11. Press "Power" button to turn on the unit. 12. Then press "GELATO" button. 13. When the program is completed, with a spoon, create a 1½-inch wide hole in the center that reaches the bottom of the pint container. 14. Add the peanut butter Cup and peanuts into the hole and press "MIX-IN" button. 15. When the program is completed, turn the outer bowl and release it from the machine. 16. Transfer the gelato into serving bowls and serve immediately.

Marshmallow Gelato

Prep time: 20 minutes | Cook time: 5 minutes | Serves 4

1 cup whole milk
½ cup heavy cream
¼ cup sugar
3 egg yolk
Pinch of sea salt
¼ cup mini marshmallows

1. Preheat the oven to broiler. Lightly grease a baking sheet. 2. Arrange the marshmallows onto the prepared baking sheet in a single layer. 3. Broil for about 5 minutes, flipping once halfway through. 4. Meanwhile, in a small saucepan, add the milk, heavy cream, sugar, egg yolks and a pinch of salt and beat until well combined. 5. Place the saucepan over medium heat and cook for about 1 minute, stirring continuously. 6. Remove from the heat and stir in half of the marshmallows. 7. Transfer the mixture into an empty Ninja CREAMi pint container. 8. Place the container into an ice bath to cool. 9. After cooling, cover the container with the storage lid and freeze for 24 hours. 10. Reserve the remaining marshmallows into the freezer. 11. After 24 hours, remove the lid from container and arrange into the outer bowl of Ninja CREAMi. 12. Install the "Creamerizer Paddle" onto the lid of outer bowl. 13. Then rotate the lid clockwise to lock. 14. Press "Power" button to turn on the unit. 15. Then press "GELATO" button. 16. When the program is completed, with a spoon, create a 1½-inch wide hole in the center that reaches the bottom of the pint container. 17. Add the reserved frozen marshmallows into the hole and press "MIX-IN" button. 18. When the program is completed, turn the outer bowl and release it from the machine. 19. Transfer the gelato into serving bowls and serve immediately.

Squash Gelato

Prep time: 5 minutes | Cook time: 5 minutes | Serves 4

1¾ cups milk
½ cup cooked butternut squash
¼ cup granulated sugar
½ teaspoon ground cinnamon
¼ teaspoon ground allspice
Pinch of salt

1. In a small saucepan, add all ingredients and beat until well combined. 2. Place the saucepan over medium heat and cook for about 5 minutes, stirring continuously. 3. Remove from the heat and transfer the mixture into an empty Ninja CREAMi pint container. 4. Place the container into an ice bath to cool. 5. After cooling, cover the container with the storage lid and freeze for 24 hours. 6. After 24 hours, remove the lid from container and arrange into the outer bowl of Ninja CREAMi. 7. Install the "Creamerizer Paddle" onto the lid of outer bowl. 8. Then rotate the lid clockwise to lock. 9. Press "Power" button to turn on the unit. 10. Then press "GELATO" button. 11. When the program is completed, turn the outer bowl and release it from the machine. 12. Transfer the gelato into serving bowls and serve immediately.

Carrot Gelato

Prep time: 5 minutes | Cook time: 3 minutes | Serves 4

- 3 large egg yolks
- ⅓ cup coconut sugar
- 1 tablespoon brown rice syrup
- ½ cup heavy cream
- 1 cup unsweetened almond milk
- ½ cup carrot puree
- ½ teaspoon ground cinnamon
- ¼ teaspoon ground nutmeg
- ¼ teaspoon ground ginger
- ¼ teaspoon ground cloves
- ¾ teaspoon vanilla extract

1. In a small saucepan, add the egg yolks, coconut sugar and brown rice syrup and beat until well combined. 2. Add the heavy cream, almond milk, carrot puree and spices and beat until well combined. 3. Place the saucepan over medium heat and cook for about 2-3 minutes, stirring continuously. 4. Remove from the heat and stir in the vanilla extract. 5. Through a fine-mesh strainer, strain the mixture into an empty Ninja CREAMi pint container. 6. Place the container into an ice bath to cool. 7. After cooling, cover the container with the storage lid and freeze for 24 hours. 8. After 24 hours, remove the lid from container and arrange into the outer bowl of Ninja CREAMi. 9. Install the "Creamerizer Paddle" onto the lid of outer bowl. 10. Then rotate the lid clockwise to lock. 11. Press "Power" button to turn on the unit. 12. Then press "GELATO" button. 13. When the program is completed, turn the outer bowl and release it from the machine. 14. Transfer the gelato into serving bowls and serve immediately.

Red Velvet Gelato

Prep time: 5 minutes | Cook time: 3 minutes | Serves 4

- 4 large egg yolks
- ¼ cup granulated sugar
- 2 tablespoons unsweetened cocoa powder
- 1 cup whole milk
- ⅓ cup heavy (whipping) cream
- ¼ cup cream cheese, at room temperature
- 1 teaspoon vanilla extract
- 1 teaspoon red food coloring

1. Fill a large bowl with ice water and set it aside. 2. In a small saucepan, whisk together the egg yolks, sugar, and cocoa powder until everything is fully combined and the sugar is dissolved. Do not do this over heat. 3. Whisk in the milk, heavy cream, cream cheese, vanilla, and food coloring. 4. Place the pan over medium heat. Cook, stirring constantly with a rubber spatula, until the temperature reaches 165°F to 175°F on an instant-read thermometer. 5. Remove the pan from the heat and pour the base through a fine-mesh strainer into a clean CREAMi Pint. Carefully place the container in the prepared ice water bath, making sure the water doesn't spill into the base. 6. Once the base has cooled, place the storage lid on the pint and freeze for 24 hours. 7. Remove the pint from the freezer and take off the lid. Place the pint in the outer bowl of your Ninja CREAMi, install the Creamerizer Paddle in the outer bowl lid, and lock the lid assembly onto the outer bowl. Place the bowl assembly on the motor base, and twist the handle to the right to raise the platform and lock it in place. Select the Gelato function. 8. Once the machine has finished processing, remove the gelato from the pint. Serve immediately.

Pumpkin Gelato

Prep time: 5 minutes | Cook time: 3 minutes | Serves 4

- 3 large egg yolks
- ⅓ cup granulated sugar
- 1 tablespoon light corn syrup
- 1 cup whole milk
- ½ cup heavy cream
- ½ cup canned pumpkin puree
- 1½ teaspoons pumpkin pie spice
- 1 teaspoon vanilla extract

1. In a small saucepan, add the egg yolks, sugar and corn syrup and beat until well combined. 2. Add the milk, heavy cream, pumpkin puree and pumpkin pie spice and beat until well combined. 3. Place the saucepan over medium heat and cook for about 2-3 minutes, stirring continuously. 4. Remove from the heat and stir in the vanilla extract. 5. Through a fine-mesh strainer, strain the mixture into an empty Ninja CREAMi pint container. 6. Place the container into an ice bath to cool. 7. After cooling, cover the container with the storage lid and freeze for 24 hours. 8. After 24 hours, remove the lid from container and arrange into the outer bowl of Ninja CREAMi. 9. Install the "Creamerizer Paddle" onto the lid of outer bowl. 10. Then rotate the lid clockwise to lock. 11. Press "Power" button to turn on the unit. 12. Then press "GELATO" button. 13. When the program is completed, turn the outer bowl and release it from the machine. 14. Transfer the gelato into serving bowls and serve immediately.

Vanilla Bean Gelato

Prep time: 5 minutes | Cook time: 3 minutes | Serves 4

- 4 large egg yolks
- 1 tablespoon light corn syrup
- ¼ cup plus 1 tablespoon granulated sugar
- ⅓ cup whole milk
- 1 cup heavy (whipping) cream
- 1 whole vanilla bean, split in half lengthwise and scraped

1. Fill a large bowl with ice water and set it aside. 2. In a small saucepan, whisk together the egg yolks, corn syrup, and sugar until everything is fully combined and the sugar is dissolved. Do not do this over heat. 3. Whisk in the milk, heavy cream, and vanilla bean scrapings (discard the pod). 4. Place the pan over medium heat. Cook, stirring constantly with a rubber spatula, until the temperature reaches 165°F to 175°F on an instant-read thermometer. 5. Remove the pan from the heat and pour the base through a fine-mesh strainer into a clean CREAMi Pint. Carefully place the container in the prepared ice water bath, making sure the water doesn't spill into the base. 6. Once the base has cooled, place the storage lid on the pint and freeze for 24 hours. 7. Remove the pint from the freezer and take off the lid. Place the pint in the outer bowl of your Ninja CREAMi, install the Creamerizer Paddle in the outer bowl lid, and lock the lid assembly onto the outer bowl. Place the bowl assembly on the motor base, and twist the handle to the right to raise the platform and lock it in place. Select the Gelato function. 8. Once the machine has finished processing, remove the gelato from the pint. Serve immediately with desired toppings.

Tiramisu Gelato

Prep time: 15 minutes | Cook time: 6 minutes | Serves 4

4 large egg yolks	¼ cup cream cheese
⅓ cup granulated sugar	1 tablespoon instant coffee
1 cup whole milk	1 teaspoon rum extract
⅓ cup heavy (whipping) cream	¼ cup ladyfinger pieces

1. Fill a large bowl with ice water and set it aside. 2. In a small saucepan, whisk together the egg yolks and sugar until the mixture is fully combined and the sugar is dissolved. Do not do this over heat. 3. Whisk in the milk, heavy cream, cream cheese, instant coffee, and rum extract. 4. Place the pan over medium heat. Cook, stirring constantly with a rubber spatula, until the temperature reaches 165°F to 175°F on an instant-read thermometer. 5. Remove the pan from the heat and pour the base through a fine-mesh strainer into a clean CREAMi Pint. Carefully place the container in the prepared ice water bath, making sure the water doesn't spill into the base. 6. Once the base has cooled, place the storage lid on the pint and freeze for 24 hours. 7. Remove the pint from the freezer and take off the lid. Place the pint in the outer bowl of your Ninja CREAMi, install the Creamerizer Paddle in the outer bowl lid, and lock the lid assembly onto the outer bowl. Place the bowl assembly on the motor base, and twist the handle to the right to raise the platform and lock it in place. Select the Gelato function. 8. Once the machine has finished processing, remove the lid from the pint container. With a spoon, create a 1½-inch-wide hole that reaches the bottom of the pint. During this process, it is okay if your treat reaches above the Max Fill line. Add the ladyfinger pieces to the hole in the pint, replace the lid, and select the Mix-In function. 9. Once the machine has finished processing, remove the gelato from the pint. Serve immediately.

Blueberry & Crackers Gelato

Prep time: 10 minutes | Cook time: 3 minutes | Serves 4

4 large egg yolks	⅓ cup heavy cream
3 tablespoons granulated sugar	¼ cup cream cheese, softened
3 tablespoons wild blueberry preserves	3-6 drops purple food coloring
1 teaspoon vanilla extract	2 large graham crackers, broken in 1-inch pieces
1 cup whole milk	

1. In a small saucepan, add the egg yolks, sugar, blueberry preserves and vanilla extract and beat until well combined. 2. Add the milk, heavy cream, cream cheese and food coloring and beat until well combined. 3. Place the saucepan over medium heat and cook for about 2-3 minutes, stirring continuously. 4. Remove from the heat and through a fine-mesh strainer, strain the mixture into an empty Ninja CREAMi pint container. 5. Place the container into an ice bath to cool. 6. After cooling, cover the container with the storage lid and freeze for 24 hours. 7. After 24 hours, remove the lid from container and arrange into the outer bowl of Ninja CREAMi. 8. Install the "Creamerizer Paddle" onto the lid of outer bowl. 9. Then rotate the lid clockwise to lock. 10. Press "Power" button to turn on the unit. 11. Then press "GELATO" button. 12. When the program is completed, with a spoon, create a 1½-inch wide hole in the center that reaches the bottom of the pint container. 13. Add the graham crackers into the hole and press "MIX-IN" button. 14. When the program is completed, turn the outer bowl and release it from the machine. 15. Transfer the gelato into serving bowls and serve immediately.

Spirulina Cookie Gelato

Prep time: 5 minutes | Cook time: 3 minutes | Serves 4

4 large egg yolks	1 teaspoon blue spirulina powder
⅓ cup granulated sugar	
1 up oat milk	4 small crunchy chocolate chip cookies, crumbled
1 teaspoon vanilla extract	

1. In a small saucepan, add the egg yolks and sugar and beat until well combined. 2. Add oat milk and vanilla extract and stir to combine. 3. Place the saucepan over medium heat and cook for about 2-3 minutes, stirring continuously. 4. Remove from the heat and through a fine-mesh strainer, strain the mixture into an empty Ninja CREAMi pint container. 5. Place the container into an ice bath to cool. 6. After cooling, cover the container with the storage lid and freeze for 24 hours. 7. After 24 hours, remove the lid from container and arrange into the outer bowl of Ninja CREAMi. 8. Install the "Creamerizer Paddle" onto the lid of outer bowl. 9. Then rotate the lid clockwise to lock. 10. Press "Power" button to turn on the unit. 11. Then press "GELATO" button. 12. When the program is completed, with a spoon, create a 1½-inch wide hole in the center that reaches the bottom of the pint container. 13. Add the chocolate chip cookies into the hole and press "MIX-IN" button. 14. When the program is completed, turn the outer bowl and release it from the machine. 15. Transfer the gelato into serving bowls and serve immediately.

Pecan Gelato

Prep time: 10 minutes | Cook time: 3 minutes | Serves 4

4 large egg yolks
5 tablespoons granulated sugar
1 tablespoon light corn syrup
1 cup heavy cream

⅓ cup whole milk
1 teaspoon butter flavor extract
⅓ cup pecans, chopped

1. In a small saucepan, add the egg yolks, sugar and corn syrup and beat until well combined. 2. Add the heavy cream, milk and butter flavor extract and beat until well combined. 3. Place the saucepan over medium heat and cook for about 2-3 minutes, stirring continuously. 4. Remove from the heat and through a fine-mesh strainer, strain the mixture into an empty Ninja CREAMi pint container. 5. Place the container into an ice bath to cool. 6. After cooling, cover the container with the storage lid and freeze for 24 hours. 7. After 24 hours, remove the lid from container and arrange into the outer bowl of Ninja CREAMi. 8. Install the "Creamerizer Paddle" onto the lid of outer bowl. 9. Then rotate the lid clockwise to lock. 10. Press "Power" button to turn on the unit. 11. Then press "GELATO" button. 12. When the program is completed, with a spoon, create a 1½-inch wide hole in the center that reaches the bottom of the pint container. 13. Add the pecans into the hole and press "MIX-IN" button. 14. When the program is completed, turn the outer bowl and release it from the machine. 15. Transfer the gelato into serving bowls and serve immediately.

Caramel Egg Gelato

Prep time: 15 minutes | Cook time: 10 minutes | Serves 4

¼ cup agave nectar
¾ cup unsweetened soy milk
½ cup unsweetened creamer

2 eggs
3 tablespoons granulated sugar
¼ cup caramels, chopped

1. In a medium saucepan, add agave nectar over medium-high heat and cook for about 2-3 minutes. 2. Remove the saucepan from heat and slowly whisk in the soy milk and creamer. 3. Return the pan over medium-high heat and whisk in the eggs and sugar. 4. Cook for about 4-5 minutes, stirring frequently. 5. Remove from the heat and through a fine-mesh strainer, strain the mixture into an empty Ninja CREAMi pint container. 6. Place the container into an ice bath to cool. 7. After cooling, cover the container with the storage lid and freeze for 24 hours. 8. After 24 hours, remove the lid from container and arrange into the outer bowl of Ninja CREAMi. 9. Install the "Creamerizer Paddle" onto the lid of outer bowl. 10. Then rotate the lid clockwise to lock. 11. Press "Power" button to turn on the unit. 12. Then press "GELATO" button. 13. When the program is completed, with a spoon, create a 1½-inch wide hole in the center that reaches the bottom of the pint container. 14. Add the chopped caramels into the hole and press "MIX-IN" button. 15. When the program is completed, turn the outer bowl and release it from the machine. 16. Transfer the gelato into serving bowls and serve immediately.

Chapter 5 Smoothie Bowls Recipes

Chapter 5 Smoothie Bowls Recipes

Strawberry-orange Creme Smoothie

Prep time: 5 minutes | Cook time: 5 minutes | Serves 1

1 container Yoplait Greek 100 orange creme yogurt
½ cup fresh strawberries, hulled
¼ cup ice cubes (optional)
¼ cup orange juice

1. Put all the ingredients into an empty ninja CREAMi Pint. 2. Place the Ninja CREAMi Pint into the outer bowl. Place the outer bowl with the Pint in it into the ninja CREAMi machine and turn until the outer bowl locks into place. Push the SMOOTHIE button. During the SMOOTHIE function, the ingredients will mix together and become very creamy. 3. Once the SMOOTHIE function has ended, turn the outer bowl and release it from the ninja CREAMi machine. 4. Scoop the smoothie into a tall glass.

Raspberry & Mango Smoothie Bowl

Prep time: 5 minutes | Cook time: 3 minutes | Serves 2

¾ cup frozen mango chunks
½ cup frozen raspberries
½ cup whole milk Greek yogurt
2 tablespoons avocado flesh
1 tablespoon agave nectar

1. In a large bowl, add all the ingredients and mix well. 2. Transfer the mixture into an empty Ninja CREAMi pint container. 3. Cover the container with the storage lid and freeze for 24 hours. 4. After 24 hours, remove the lid from container and arrange into the outer bowl of Ninja CREAMi. 5. Install the "Creamerizer Paddle" onto the lid of outer bowl. 6. Then rotate the lid clockwise to lock. 7. Press "Power" button to turn on the unit. 8. Then press "SMOOTHIE BOWL" button. 9. When the program is completed, turn the outer bowl and release it from the machine. 10. Transfer the smoothie into serving bowls and serve immediately.

Vanilla Pumpkin Pie Smoothie

Prep time: 5 minutes | Cook time: 10 minutes | Serves 1

4 ounces pumpkin pie filling (such as Libby's)
½ cup vanilla frozen yogurt
¼ cup ice
¼ cup vanilla-flavored soy milk
½ teaspoon ground cinnamon
1 pinch ground nutmeg
⅛ teaspoon vanilla extract

1. Combine the pumpkin pie filling, frozen yogurt, ice, soy milk, cinnamon, nutmeg, and vanilla extract and put into an empty ninja CREAMi Pint. 2. Place the Ninja CREAMi Pint into the outer bowl. Place the outer bowl with the Pint in it into the ninja CREAMi machine and turn until the outer bowl locks into place. Push the SMOOTHIE button. During the SMOOTHIE function, the ingredients will mix together and become very creamy. 3. Once the SMOOTHIE function has ended, turn the outer bowl and release it from the ninja CREAMi machine. 4. Pour the smoothie into a glass.

Pumpkin & Banana Smoothie Bowl

Prep time: 5 minutes | Cook time: 3 minutes | Serves 2

1 cup canned pumpkin puree
⅓ cup plain Greek yogurt
1½ tablespoons maple syrup
1 teaspoon vanilla extract
1 teaspoon pumpkin pie spice
1 frozen banana, peeled and cut in ½-inch pieces

1. In an empty Ninja CREAMi pint container, add the pumpkin puree, yogurt, maple syrup, vanilla extract, and pumpkin pie spice and mix well. 2. Add the banana pieces and stir to combine. 3. Transfer the mixture into an empty Ninja CREAMi pint container. 4. Arrange the container into the outer bowl of Ninja CREAMi. 5. Install the "Creamerizer Paddle" onto the lid of outer bowl. 6. Then rotate the lid clockwise to lock. 7. Press "Power" button to turn on the unit. 8. Then press "SMOOTHIE BOWL" button. 9. When the program is completed, turn the outer bowl and release it from the machine. 10. Transfer the smoothie into serving bowls and serve immediately.

Gator Smoothies

Prep time: 5 minutes | Cook time: 5 minutes | Serves 1

1 cup ice
1 cup grape-flavored sports drink
1 scoop vanilla ice cream

1. Add the ice, sports drink, and ice cream into an empty ninja CREAMi Pint. 2. Place the Ninja CREAMi Pint into the outer bowl. Place the outer bowl with the Pint in it into the ninja CREAMi machine and turn until the outer bowl locks into place. Push the SMOOTHIE button. During the SMOOTHIE function, the ingredients will mix together and become very creamy. 3. Once the SMOOTHIE function has ended, turn the outer bowl and release it from the ninja CREAMi machine. 4. Pour into a tall glass.

Crazy Fruit Smoothie

Prep time: 5 minutes | Cook time: 10 minutes | Serves 1

- 1 cup crushed ice
- 1 banana, chopped
- 1 kiwi, peeled and chopped
- ½ cup chopped strawberries
- ½ cup chopped pineapple
- ¼ cup cream of coconut
- 1 tablespoon coconut flakes, for garnish

1. Add the ice, banana, kiwi, strawberries, pineapple, and cream of coconut into an empty ninja CREAMi Pint 2. Place the Ninja CREAMi Pint into the outer bowl. Place the outer bowl with the Pint in it into the ninja CREAMi machine and turn until the outer bowl locks into place. Push the SMOOTHIE button. During the SMOOTHIE function, the ingredients will mix together and become very creamy. 3. Once the SMOOTHIE function has ended, turn the outer bowl and release it from the ninja CREAMi machine. 4. Pour the smoothie into a tall glass.

Kale, Avocado & Fruit Smoothie Bowl

Prep time: 5 minutes | Cook time: 3 minutes | Serves 4

- 1 banana, peeled and cut into 1-inch pieces
- ½ of avocado, peeled, pitted and cut into 1-inch pieces
- 1 cup fresh kale leaves
- 1 cup green apple, peeled, cored and cut into 1-inch pieces
- ¼ cup unsweetened coconut milk
- 2 tablespoons agave nectar

1. In a large high-speed blender, add all the ingredients and pulse until smooth. 2. Transfer the mixture into an empty Ninja CREAMi pint container. 3. Cover the container with storage lid and freeze for 24 hours. 4. After 24 hours, remove the lid from container and arrange into the Outer Bowl of Ninja CREAMi. 5. Install the Creamerizer Paddle onto the lid of Outer Bowl. 6. Then rotate the lid clockwise to lock. 7. Press Power button to turn on the unit. 8. Then press Smoothie Bowl button. 9. When the program is completed, turn the Outer Bowl and release it from the machine. 10. Transfer the smoothie into serving bowls and serve immediately.

Coffee Smoothie Bowl

Prep time: 5 minutes | Cook time: 3 minutes | Serves 2

- 2 cups unsweetened vanilla almond milk
- ¼ cup instant coffee

1. In a large bowl, add the almond milk and instant coffee mix and beat until well combine 2. Transfer the mixture into an empty Ninja CREAMi pint container. 3. Cover the container with storage lid and freeze for 24 hours. 4. After 24 hours, remove the lid from container and arrange into the Outer Bowl of Ninja CREAMi. 5. Install the Creamerizer Paddle onto the lid of Outer Bowl. 6. Then rotate the lid clockwise to lock. 7. Press Power button to turn on the unit. 8. Then press Smoothie Bowl button. 9. When the program is completed, turn the Outer Bowl and release it from the machine. 10. Transfer the smoothie into serving bowls and serve immediately.

Chocolate Pumpkin Smoothie Bowl

Prep time: 5 minutes | Cook time: 3 minutes | Serves 4

- ½ cup canned pumpkin puree
- 2 tablespoons unsweetened cocoa powder
- 1 teaspoon pumpkin spice seasoning
- 2 ripe bananas, cut in ½-inch pieces
- 1 tablespoon agave nectar
- ¼ cup whole milk

1. In a small bowl, stir together the pumpkin puree, cocoa powder, and pumpkin spice until well combined. Pour the base into a clean CREAMi Pint. Mix in the bananas, agave, and milk until everything is fully combined and the bananas are coated. Place the storage lid on the container and freeze for 24 hours. 2. Remove the pint from the freezer and take off the lid. Place the pint in the outer bowl of your Ninja CREAMi, install the Creamerizer Paddle in the outer bowl lid, and lock the lid assembly onto the outer bowl. Place the bowl assembly on the motor base, and twist the handle to the right to raise the platform and lock it in place. Select the Smoothie Bowl function. 3. Once the machine has finished processing, remove the smoothie bowl from the pint. Serve immediately with your desired toppings.

Avocado & Banana Smoothie Bowl

Prep time: 5 minutes | Cook time: 5 minutes | Serves 4

- ½ cup unsweetened coconut milk
- ¼ cup fresh apple juice
- 2 tablespoons whey protein isolate
- 4-5 tablespoons maple syrup
- ¼ teaspoon vanilla extract
- 1 cup ripe avocado, peeled, pitted and cut in ½-inch pieces
- 1 cup fresh banana, peeled and cut in ½-inch pieces

1. In a large bowl, add the coconut milk, apple juice, protein isolate, maple syrup and vanilla extract and beat until well combined. 2. Place the avocado and banana into an empty Ninja CREAMi pint container and with the back of a spoon, firmly press the fruit below the MAX FILL line. 3. Top with coconut milk mixture and mix until well combined. 4. Cover the container with the storage lid and freeze for 24 hours. 5. After 24 hours, remove the lid from container and arrange into the outer bowl of Ninja CREAMi. 6. Install the "Creamerizer Paddle" onto the lid of outer bowl. 7. Then rotate the lid clockwise to lock. 8. Press "Power" button to turn on the unit. 9. Then press "SMOOTHIE BOWL" button. 10. When the program is completed, turn the outer bowl and release it from the machine. 11. Transfer the smoothie into serving bowls and serve immediately.

Green Monster Smoothie

Prep time: 5 minutes | Cook time: 10 minutes | Serves 1

- ½ cup baby spinach
- ½ apple, peeled, cored, and chopped
- ½ banana, sliced
- ¼ cup chopped carrots
- ¼ cup orange juice
- ¼ cup fresh strawberries
- ¼ cup ice

1. Put the spinach, apples, bananas, carrots, orange juice, strawberries, and ice into an empty ninja CREAMi Pint. 2. Place the Ninja CREAMi Pint into the outer bowl. Place the outer bowl with the Pint in it into the ninja CREAMi machine and turn until the outer bowl locks into place. Push the SMOOTHIE button. During the SMOOTHIE function, the ingredients will mix together and become very creamy. 3. Once the SMOOTHIE function has ended, turn the outer bowl and release it from the ninja CREAMi machine. 4. Scoop the smoothie into a glass.

Chocolate Fudge Frosting

Prep time: 5 minutes | Cook time: 5 minutes | Serves 1

- ½ cup cold unsalted butter, cut in 8 pieces
- 1½ cups confectioners' sugar
- 2 tablespoons dark unsweetened cocoa powder
- 1 tablespoon heavy (whipping) cream
- 1 teaspoon vanilla extract

1. Place all the ingredients in a clean CREAMi Pint in the order listed. 2. Place the pint in the outer bowl of your Ninja CREAMi, install the Creamerizer Paddle in the outer bowl lid, and lock the lid assembly onto the outer bowl. Place the bowl assembly on the motor base, and twist the handle to the right to raise the platform and lock it in place. Select the Re-Spin function. 3. Once the machine has finished processing, the frosting should be smooth and easily scoopable with a spoon. If the frosting is too thick, select the Re-Spin function again and process until creamy and smooth.

Simple Smoothie Bowl

Prep time: 5 minutes | Cook time: 5 minutes | Serves 2

- 1 bottle fruit smoothie beverage

1. Pour the smoothie beverage into a clean CREAMi Pint. Place the storage lid on the container and freeze for 24 hours 2. Remove the pint from the freezer and take off the lid. Place the pint in the outer bowl of your Ninja CREAMi, install the Creamerizer Paddle in the outer bowl lid, and lock the lid assembly onto the outer bowl. Place the bowl assembly on the motor base, and twist the handle to the right to raise the platform and lock it in place. Select the Smoothie Bowl function. 3. Once the machine has finished processing, remove the smoothie bowl from the pint. Serve immediately with desired toppings.

Strawberry Smoothie Bowl

Prep time: 5 minutes | Cook time: 5 minutes | Serves 4

- 2 tablespoons vanilla protein powder
- ¼ cup agave nectar
- ¼ cup pineapple juice
- ½ cup whole milk
- 1 cup ripe banana, peeled and cut in ½-inch pieces
- 1 cup fresh strawberries, hulled and quartered

1. In a large bowl, add the protein powder, agave nectar, pineapple juice and milk and beat until well combined. 2. Place the banana and strawberry into an empty Ninja CREAMi pint container and with the back of a spoon, firmly press the fruit below the Max Fill line. 3. Top with milk mixture and mix until well combined. 4. Cover the container with storage lid and freeze for 24 hours. 5. After 24 hours, remove the lid from container and arrange into the Outer Bowl of Ninja CREAMi. 6. Install the Creamerizer Paddle onto the lid of Outer Bowl. 7. Then rotate the lid clockwise to lock. 8. Press Power button to turn on the unit. 9. Then press Smoothie Bowl button. 10. When the program is completed, turn the Outer Bowl and release it from the machine. 11. Transfer the smoothie into serving bowls and serve immediately.

Microwave Vanilla Cake

Prep time: 5 minutes | Cook time: 5 minutes | Serves 2

- ½ teaspoon vanilla extract
- 3 tablespoons whole milk
- 2 tablespoons unsalted butter
- ⅛ teaspoon kosher salt
- ½ teaspoon baking powder
- 2 tablespoons granulated sugar
- ¼ cup all-purpose flour
- Chocolate Fudge Frosting, for serving (optional)

1. Place all the ingredients except for the frosting in a clean CREAMi Pint container in the order listed. 2. Place the pint in the outer bowl of your Ninja CREAMi, install the Creamerizer Paddle in the outer bowl lid, and lock the lid assembly onto the outer bowl. Place the bowl assembly on the motor base, and twist the handle to the right to raise the platform and lock it in place. Select the Re-Spin function. 3. Once the machine has finished processing, place the pint container in the microwave and cook on High for 2 minutes. Check the cake for doneness—a skewer or knife inserted into the cake should come out clean, and the cake should pull away from the sides of the pint container. 4. Once the container is cool enough to handle, run a butter knife around the inside of the pint. Flip the pint over, and the cake should pop right out. 5. If you want to add frosting, slice the cake widthwise into 3 layers. Place one slice on a plate and frost the top of the layer. Lay a second slice on top of the first and frost the top. Top with the final slice of cake, then frost the top and sides of the assembled cake. 6. Cut in half and serve.

Vodka Smoothie

Prep time: 5 minutes | Cook time: 5 minutes | Serves 2

3 fluid ounces vodka
9 fluid ounces orange juice
½ cup frozen strawberries
2 scoops orange sherbet
½ cup crushed ice

1. Mix the vodka, orange juice, strawberries, orange sherbet, and ice in an empty ninja CREAMi Pint. 2. Place the Ninja CREAMi Pint into the outer bowl. Place the outer bowl with the Pint in it into the ninja CREAMi machine and turn until the outer bowl locks into place. Push the SMOOTHIE button. During the SMOOTHIE function, the ingredients will mix together and become very creamy. 3. Once the SMOOTHIE function has ended, turn the outer bowl and release it from the ninja CREAMi machine. 4. Scoop the smoothie into glass cups.

Peaches And Cream Smoothie Bowl

Prep time: 5 minutes | Cook time: 3 minutes | Serves 4

1 can peaches in their juice
¼ cup vanilla yogurt
2 tablespoons agave nectar

1. Place the peaches in their juice, yogurt, and agave in a clean CREAMi Pint and stir to combine. Place the storage lid on the container and freeze for 24 hours. 2. Remove the pint from the freezer and take off the lid. Place the pint in the outer bowl of your Ninja CREAMi, install the Creamerizer Paddle in the outer bowl lid, and lock the lid assembly onto the outer bowl. Place the bowl assembly on the motor base, and twist the handle to the right to raise the platform and lock it in place. Select the Smoothie Bowl function. 3. Once the machine has finished processing, remove the smoothie bowl from the pint. Serve immediately with desired toppings.

Fruity Coffee Smoothie Bowl

Prep time: 5 minutes | Cook time: 3 minutes | Serves 4

1 cup brewed coffee
½ cup oat milk
2 tablespoons almond butter
1 cup fresh raspberries
1 large banana, peeled and sliced

1. In a high-speed blender add all the ingredients and pulse until smooth. 2. Transfer the mixture into an empty Ninja CREAMi pint container. 3. Cover the container with the storage lid and freeze for 24 hours. 4. After 24 hours, remove the lid from container and arrange into the outer bowl of Ninja CREAMi. 5. Install the "Creamerizer Paddle" onto the lid of outer bowl. 6. Then rotate the lid clockwise to lock. 7. Press "Power" button to turn on the unit. 8. Then press "SMOOTHIE BOWL" button. 9. When the program is completed, turn the outer bowl and release it from the machine. 10. Transfer the smoothie into serving bowls and serve immediately.

Buttery Coffee Smoothie

Prep time: 5 minutes | Cook time: 5 minutes | Serves 1

1 cup brewed coffee
2 large pasteurized egg yolks
¼ cup avocado
¼ cup ice cubes
1 tablespoon coconut sugar
2 tablespoons coconut oil, melted

1. Combine the coffee, egg yolks, avocado, ice cubes, and coconut sugar in an empty ninja CREAMi Pint. 2. Place the Ninja CREAMi Pint into the outer bowl. Place the outer bowl with the Pint in it into the ninja CREAMi machine and turn until the outer bowl locks into place. Push the SMOOTHIE button. During the SMOOTHIE function, the ingredients will mix together and become very creamy. 3. Once the SMOOTHIE function has ended, turn the outer bowl and release it from the ninja CREAMi machine. 4. Scoop the smoothie into a tall glass.

Avocado Smoothie

Prep time: 5 minutes | Cook time: 5 minutes | Serves 1

½ ripe avocado, peeled, halved, and pitted
½ cup milk
¼ cup vanilla yogurt
1½ tablespoons honey
4 ice cubes

1. Combine the avocado, milk, yogurt, honey, and ice cubes in an empty ninja CREAMi Pint. 2. Place the Ninja CREAMi Pint into the outer bowl. Place the outer bowl with the Pint in it into the ninja CREAMi machine and turn until the outer bowl locks into place. Push the SMOOTHIE button. During the SMOOTHIE function, the ingredients will mix together and become very creamy. 3. Once the SMOOTHIE function has ended, turn the outer bowl and release it from the ninja CREAMi machine. 4. Pour the smoothie into glasses.

Dragon Fruit & Pineapple Smoothie Bowl

Prep time: 5 minutes | Cook time: 5 minutes | Serves 4

2 cups frozen dragon fruit chunks
2 cans pineapple juice

1. Place the dragon fruit chunks into an empty Ninja CREAMi pint container. 2. Top with pineapple juice and stir to combine. 3. Cover the container with storage lid and freeze for 24 hours. 4. After 24 hours, remove the lid from container and arrange into the Outer Bowl of Ninja CREAMi. 5. Install the Creamerizer Paddle onto the lid of Outer Bowl. 6. Then rotate the lid clockwise to lock. 7. Press Power button to turn on the unit. 8. Then press Smoothie Bowl button. 9. When the program is completed, turn the Outer Bowl and release it from the machine. 10. Transfer the smoothie into serving bowls and serve immediately.

Piescream

Prep time: 5 minutes | Cook time: 5 minutes | Serves 4

- 1 can cherry pie filling
- 1 store-bought frozen graham cracker crust
- 1 container whipped topping

1. Fill a clean CREAMi Pint to the max fill line with the pie filing. Place the storage lid on the container and freeze for 24 hours. 2. Remove the pint from the freezer and take off the lid. Place the pint in the outer bowl of your Ninja CREAMi, install the Creamerizer Paddle in the outer bowl lid, and lock the lid assembly onto the outer bowl. Place the bowl assembly on the motor base, and twist the handle to the right to raise the platform and lock it in place. Select the Sorbet function. 3. Once the machine has finished processing, remove the sorbet from the pint. Let it thaw until it is spreadable, about 5 minutes. 4. Spread the pie filling sorbet onto the frozen graham cracker crust. Spread the whipped topping on top of the filling. Freeze for 4 to 6 hours or until hardened. When ready to serve, remove from the freezer. Let the pie thaw just until you can slice it with a knife.

Mixed Berries Smoothie Bowl

Prep time: 5 minutes | Cook time: 5 minutes | Serves 4

- ¾ cup fresh strawberries, hulled and quartered
- ¾ cup fresh raspberries
- ¾ cup fresh blueberries
- ¾ cup fresh blackberries
- ¼ cup plain Greek yogurt
- 1 tablespoon honey

1. In an empty Ninja CREAMi pint container, place the berries and with the back of a spoon, firmly press the berries below the Max Fill line. 2. Add the yogurt and honey and stir to combine. 3. Cover the container with storage lid and freeze for 24 hours. 4. After 24 hours, remove the lid from container and arrange into the Outer Bowl of Ninja CREAMi. 5. Install the Creamerizer Paddle onto the lid of Outer Bowl. 6. Then rotate the lid clockwise to lock. 7. Press Power button to turn on the unit. 8. Then press Smoothie Bowl button. 9. When the program is completed, turn the Outer Bowl and release it from the machine. 10. Transfer the smoothie into serving bowls and serve immediately.

Mango Smoothie Bowl

Prep time: 5 minutes | Cook time: 5 minutes | Serves 4

- 2 cups ripe mango, peeled, pitted and cut into 1-inch pieces
- 1 can of unsweetened coconut milk

1. Place the mango pieces into an empty Ninja CREAMi pint container. 2. Top with coconut milk and stir to combine. 3. Cover the container with storage lid and freeze for 24 hours. 4. After 24 hours, remove the lid from container and arrange into the Outer Bowl of Ninja CREAMi. 5. Install the Creamerizer Paddle onto the lid of Outer Bowl. 6. Then rotate the lid clockwise to lock. 7. Press Power button to turn on the unit. 8. Then press Smoothie Bowl button. 9. When the program is completed, turn the Outer Bowl and release it from the machine. 10. Transfer the smoothie into serving bowls and serve immediately.

Fruity Coconut Smoothie Bowl

Prep time: 5 minutes | Cook time: 5 minutes | Serves 2

- ½ of ripe banana, peeled and cut in ½-inch pieces
- ¼ cup coconut rum
- ¼ cup unsweetened coconut cream
- ½ cup unsweetened canned coconut milk
- ¾ cup pineapple juice
- 2 tablespoons fresh lime juice

1. In a large bowl, add all the ingredients and beat until well combined. 2. Transfer the mixture into an empty Ninja CREAMi pint container. 3. Cover the container with the storage lid and freeze for 24 hours. 4. After 24 hours, remove the lid from container and arrange into the outer bowl of Ninja CREAMi. 5. Install the "Creamerizer Paddle" onto the lid of outer bowl. 6. Then rotate the lid clockwise to lock. 7. Press "Power" button to turn on the unit. 8. Then press "SMOOTHIE BOWL" button. 9. When the program is completed, turn the outer bowl and release it from the machine. 10. Transfer the smoothie into serving bowl sand serve immediately.

Oat Banana Smoothie Bowl

Prep time: 5 minutes | Cook time: 1 minutes | Serves 2

- ½ cup water
- ¼ cup quick oats
- 1 cup vanilla Greek yogurt
- ½ cup banana, peeled and sliced
- 3 tablespoons honey

1. In a small microwave-safe bowl, add the water and oats and microwave on High or about one minute. 2. Remove from the microwave and stir in the yogurt, banana and honey until well combined. 3. Transfer the mixture into an empty Ninja CREAMi pint container. 4. Cover the container with storage lid and freeze for 24 hours. 5. After 24 hours, remove the lid from container and arrange into the Outer Bowl of Ninja CREAMi. 6. Install the Creamerizer Paddle onto the lid of Outer Bowl. 7. Then rotate the lid clockwise to lock. 8. Press Power button to turn on the unit. 9. Then press Smoothie Bowl button. 10. When the program is completed, turn the Outer Bowl and release it from the machine. 11. Transfer the smoothie into serving bowls and serve with your favorite topping.

Three Fruit Smoothie Bowl

Prep time: 5 minutes | Cook time: 3 minutes | Serves 2

1 cup frozen dragon fruit pieces	pieces
¾ cup fresh strawberries, hulled and quartered	½ cup low-fat plain yogurt
	2 tablespoons agave nectar
¾ cup pineapple, cut in 1-inch	1 tablespoon fresh lime juice

1. In a large high-speed blender, add all the ingredients and pulse until smooth. 2. Transfer the mixture into an empty Ninja CREAMi pint container. 3. Cover the container with the storage lid and freeze for 24 hours. 4. After 24 hours, remove the lid from container and arrange into the outer bowl of Ninja CREAMi. 5. Install the "Creamerizer Paddle" onto the lid of outer bowl. 6. Then rotate the lid clockwise to lock. 7. Press "Power" button to turn on the unit. 8. Then press "SMOOTHIE BOWL" button. 9. When the program is completed, turn the outer bowl and release it from the machine. 10. Transfer the smoothie into serving bowls and serve immediately.

Peach & Grapefruit Smoothie Bowl

Prep time: 5 minutes | Cook time: 3 minutes | Serves 2

1 cup frozen peach pieces	2 tablespoons honey
1 cup vanilla Greek yogurt	¼ teaspoon vanilla extract
¼ cup fresh grapefruit juice	½ teaspoon ground cinnamon

1. In a high-speed blender, add all ingredients and pulse until smooth 2. Transfer the mixture into an empty Ninja CREAMi pint container. 3. Cover the container with the storage lid and freeze for 24 hours. 4. After 24 hours, remove the lid from container and arrange into the outer bowl of Ninja CREAMi. 5. Install the "Creamerizer Paddle" onto the lid of outer bowl. 6. Then rotate the lid clockwise to lock. 7. Press "Power" button to turn on the unit. 8. Then press "SMOOTHIE BOWL" button. 9. When the program is completed, turn the outer bowl and release it from the machine. 10. Transfer the smoothie into serving bowls and serve immediately.

Kale VS Avocado Smoothie Bowl

Prep time: 5 minutes | Cook time: 3 minutes | Serves 4

1 banana, cut into 1-inch pieces	1 cup green apple pieces
½ ripe avocado, cut into 1-inch pieces	¼ cup unsweetened coconut milk
1 cup packed kale leaves	2 tablespoons agave nectar

1. Combine the banana, avocado, kale, apple, coconut milk, and agave in a blender. Blend on high for about 1 minute until smooth. 2. Pour the base into a clean CREAMi Pint. Place the storage lid on the container and freeze for 24 hours. 3. Remove the pint from the freezer and take off the lid. Place the pint in the outer bowl of your Ninja CREAMi, install the Creamerizer Paddle in the outer bowl lid, and lock the lid assembly onto the outer bowl. Place the bowl assembly on the motor base, and twist the handle to the right to raise the platform and lock it in place. Select the Smoothie Bowl function. 4. Once the machine has finished processing, remove the smoothie bowl from the pint. Serve immediately with your desired toppings.

Pumpkin Smoothie Bowl

Prep time: 5 minutes | Cook time: 5 minutes | Serves 2

1 cup canned pumpkin puree	1 teaspoon pumpkin pie spice
⅓ cup plain Greek yogurt	1 frozen banana, peeled and cut in ½-inch pieces
1½ tablespoons maple syrup	
1 teaspoon vanilla extract	

1. In an empty Ninja CREAMi pint container, add the pumpkin puree, yogurt, maple syrup, vanilla extract and pumpkin pie spice and mix well. 2. Add the banana pieces and stir to combine. 3. Transfer the mixture into an empty Ninja CREAMi pint container. 4. Arrange the container into the Outer Bowl of Ninja CREAMi. 5. Install the Creamerizer Paddle onto the lid of Outer Bowl. 6. Then rotate the lid clockwise to lock. 7. Press Power button to turn on the unit. 8. Then press Smoothie Bowl button. 9. When the program is completed, turn the Outer Bowl and release it from the machine. 10. Transfer the smoothie into serving bowls and serve immediately.

Mango & Orange Smoothie Bowl

Prep time: 5 minutes | Cook time: 3 minutes | Serves 2

1 cup frozen mango chunks	½ teaspoon ground turmeric
1 cup plain whole milk yogurt	⅛ teaspoon ground cinnamon
¼ cup fresh orange juice	⅛ teaspoon ground ginger
2 tablespoons maple syrup	Pinch of ground black pepper

1. In a high-speed blender, add all ingredients and pulse until smooth 2. Transfer the mixture into an empty Ninja CREAMi pint container. 3. Cover the container with storage lid and freeze for 24 hours. 4. After 24 hours, remove the lid from container and arrange into the Outer Bowl of Ninja CREAMi. 5. Install the Creamerizer Paddle onto the lid of Outer Bowl. 6. Then rotate the lid clockwise to lock. 7. Press Power button to turn on the unit. 8. Then press Smoothie Bowl button. 9. When the program is completed, turn the Outer Bowl and release it from the machine. 10. Transfer the smoothie into serving bowls and serve immediately.

Papaya Smoothie Bowl

Prep time: 5 minutes | Cook time: 3 minutes | Serves 2

2 cups ripe papaya, peeled and cut into 1-inch pieces	4-6 drops liquid stevia
14 ounces (397 g) whole milk	¼ teaspoon vanilla extract

1. Place the mango pieces into an empty Ninja CREAMi pint container. 2. Top with coconut milk, stevia and vanilla extract and stir to combine. 3. Cover the container with the storage lid and freeze for 24 hours. 4. After 24 hours, remove the lid from container and arrange into the outer bowl of Ninja CREAMi. 5. Install the "Creamerizer Paddle" onto the lid of outer bowl. 6. Then rotate the lid clockwise to lock. 7. Press "Power" button to turn on the unit. 8. Then press "SMOOTHIE BOWL" button. 9. When the program is completed, turn the outer bowl and release it from the machine. 10. Transfer the smoothie into serving bowls and serve immediately.

Blueberry Smoothie Bowl

Prep time: 5 minutes | Cook time: 10 minutes | Serves 1

¾ cups Ocean Spray blueberry juice cocktail, chilled	and rinsed
⅔ cup fresh blueberries, cleaned	½ cup vanilla yogurt or vanilla frozen yogurt

1. Puree the blueberries. 2. Put the pureed blueberries, blueberry juice cocktail, and yogurt into an empty ninja CREAMi Pint 3. Place the Ninja CREAMi Pint into the outer bowl. Place the outer bowl with the Pint in it into the ninja CREAMi machine and turn until the outer bowl locks into place. Push the smoothie button. During the smoothie function, the ingredients will mix together and become very creamy. 4. Once the smoothie function has ended, turn the outer bowl and release it from the ninja CREAMi machine. 5. Scoop smoothie into a bowl.

Pineapple Smoothie Bowl

Prep time: 5 minutes | Cook time: 5 minutes | Serves 4

2 ripe bananas, peeled and cut in 1-inch pieces	1 cup fresh pineapple, chopped
	¼ cup yogurt
	2 tablespoons honey

1. In a large bowl, add all the ingredients and beat until well combined. 2. Transfer the mixture into an empty Ninja CREAMi pint container. 3. Cover the container with storage lid and freeze for 24 hours. 4. After 24 hours, remove the lid from container and arrange into the Outer Bowl of Ninja CREAMi. 5. Install the Creamerizer Paddle onto the lid of Outer Bowl. 6. Then rotate the lid clockwise to lock. 7. Press Power button to turn on the unit. 8. Then press Smoothie Bowl button. 9. When the program is completed, turn the Outer Bowl and release it from the machine. 10. Transfer the smoothie into serving bowls and serve immediately.

Energy Elixir Smoothie

Prep time: 5 minutes | Cook time: 5 minutes | Serves 1

½ cup spring salad greens	pear
½ cup frozen red grapes	2 tablespoons walnuts
½ chopped frozen banana	Water as needed
½ cored and chopped frozen	

1. Layer the salad greens, red grapes, banana, pear, walnuts, and enough water to cover the mixture in an empty ninja CREAMi Pint. 2. Place the Ninja CREAMi Pint into the outer bowl. Place the outer bowl with the Pint in it into the ninja CREAMi machine and turn until the outer bowl locks into place. Push the SMOOTHIE button. During the SMOOTHIE function, the ingredients will mix together and become very creamy. 3. Once the SMOOTHIE function has ended, turn the outer bowl and release it from the ninja CREAMi machine. 4. Scoop the smoothie into a glass.

Frozen Fruit Smoothie Bowl

Prep time: 5 minutes | Cook time: 3 minutes | Serves 2

1 ripe banana, peeled and cut in 1-inch pieces	2 cups frozen fruit mix
	1¼ cups vanilla yogurt

1. In a large high-speed blender, add all the ingredients and pulse until smooth. 2. Transfer the mixture into an empty Ninja CREAMi pint container. 3. Cover the container with the storage lid and freeze for 24 hours. 4. After 24 hours, remove the lid from container and arrange into the outer bowl of Ninja CREAMi. 5. Install the "Creamerizer Paddle" onto the lid of outer bowl. 6. Then rotate the lid clockwise to lock. 7. Press "Power" button to turn on the unit. 8. Then press "SMOOTHIE BOWL" button. 9. When the program is completed, turn the outer bowl and release it from the machine. 10. Transfer the smoothie into serving bowls and serve immediately.

Raspberry Smoothie Bowl

Prep time: 5 minutes | Cook time: 3 minutes | Serves 4

1 cup brewed coffee	1 cup fresh raspberries
½ cup oat milk	1 large banana, peeled and sliced
2 tablespoons almond butter	

1. In a high-speed blender add all the ingredients and pulse until smooth. 2. Transfer the mixture into an empty Ninja CREAMi pint container. 3. Cover the container with storage lid and freeze for 24 hours. 4. After 24 hours, remove the lid from container and arrange into the Outer Bowl of Ninja CREAMi. 5. Install the Creamerizer Paddle onto the lid of Outer Bowl. 6. Then rotate the lid clockwise to lock. 7. Press Power button to turn on the unit. 8. Then press Smoothie Bowl button. 9. When the program is completed, turn the Outer Bowl and release it from the machine. 10. Transfer the smoothie into serving bowls and serve immediately.

Chocolate, Peanut Butter & Banana Smoothie

Prep time: 5 minutes | Cook time: 5 minutes | Serves 2

1 cup chocolate pudding
1 tablespoon creamy peanut butter
1 large ripe banana, cut into pieces
⅔ cup reduced-fat milk
½ cup ice cubes
Reddi-wip chocolate dairy whipped topping

1. Mash the bananas in a large bowl and add all the other ingredients except for the whipped topping. Combine and put into the ninja CREAMi Pint. 2. Place the Pint into the outer bowl. Place the outer bowl with the Pint in it into the ninja CREAMi machine and turn until the outer bowl locks into place. Push the SMOOTHIE button. The ingredients will mix together and become very creamy. 3. Once the SMOOTHIE function has ended, turn the outer bowl and release it from the ninja CREAMi machine. 4. Scoop the smoothie into glass bowls to serve.

Green Fruity Smoothie Bowl

Prep time: 5 minutes | Cook time: 5 minutes | Serves 2

1 banana, peeled and cut into 1-inch pieces
½ of avocado, peeled, pitted and cut into 1-inch pieces
1 cup fresh kale leaves
1 cup green apple, peeled, cored and cut into 1-inch pieces
¼ cup unsweetened coconut milk
2 tablespoons agave nectar

1. In a large high-speed blender, add all the ingredients and pulse until smooth. 2. Transfer the mixture into an empty Ninja CREAMi pint container. 3. Cover the container with the storage lid and freeze for 24 hours. 4. After 24 hours, remove the lid from container and arrange into the outer bowl of Ninja CREAMi. 5. Install the "Creamerizer Paddle" onto the lid of outer bowl. 6. Then rotate the lid clockwise to lock. 7. Press "Power" button to turn on the unit. 8. Then press "SMOOTHIE BOWL" button. 9. When the program is completed, turn the outer bowl and release it from the machine. 10. Transfer the smoothie into serving bowls and serve immediately.

Piña Smoothie Bowl

Prep time: 5 minutes | Cook time: 5 minutes | Serves 4

1½ cups canned pineapple chunks in their juice
½ cup canned coconut milk
1 tablespoon agave nectar

1. Pour the pineapple chunks in their juice, coconut milk, and agave into a clean CREAMi Pint and stir to combine. Place the storage lid on the container and freeze for 24 hours. 2. Remove the pint from the freezer and take off the lid. Place the pint in the outer bowl of your Ninja CREAMi, install the Creamerizer Paddle in the outer bowl lid, and lock the lid assembly onto the outer bowl. Place the bowl assembly on the motor base, and twist the handle to the right to raise the platform and lock it in place. Select the Smoothie Bowl function. 3. Once the machine has finished processing, remove the smoothie bowl from the pint. Serve immediately with your desired toppings.

Raspberry & Orange Smoothie Bowl

Prep time: 5 minutes | Cook time: 5 minutes | Serves 2

2 cups fresh raspberries
½ cup vanilla yogurt
¼ cup fresh orange juice
1 tablespoon honey

1. In an empty Ninja CREAMi pint container, place the raspberries and with the back of a spoon, firmly press the berries below the MAX FILL line. 2. Add the yogurt, orange juice and honey and stir to combine. 3. Cover the container with the storage lid and freeze for 24 hours. 4. After 24 hours, remove the lid from container and arrange into the outer bowl of Ninja CREAMi. 5. Install the "Creamerizer Paddle" onto the lid of outer bowl. 6. Then rotate the lid clockwise to lock. 7. Press "Power" button to turn on the unit. 8. Then press "SMOOTHIE BOWL" button. 9. When the program is completed, turn the outer bowl and release it from the machine. 10. Transfer the smoothie into serving bowls and serve immediately.

Orange & Mango Smoothie Bowl

Prep time: 5 minutes | Cook time: 3 minutes | Serves 2

1 cup frozen mango chunks
1 cup plain whole milk yogurt
¼ cup fresh orange juice
2 tablespoons maple syrup
½ teaspoon ground turmeric
⅛ teaspoon ground cinnamon
⅛ teaspoon ground ginger
Pinch of ground black pepper

1. In a high-speed blender, add all ingredients and pulse until smooth 2. Transfer the mixture into an empty Ninja CREAMi pint container. 3. Cover the container with the storage lid and freeze for 24 hours. 4. After 24 hours, remove the lid from container and arrange into the outer bowl of Ninja CREAMi. 5. Install the "Creamerizer Paddle" onto the lid of outer bowl. 6. Then rotate the lid clockwise to lock. 7. Press "Power" button to turn on the unit. 8. Then press "SMOOTHIE BOWL" button. 9. When the program is completed, turn the outer bowl and release it from the machine. 10. Transfer the smoothie into serving bowls and serve immediately.

Berries & Cherry Smoothie Bowl

Prep time: 5 minutes | Cook time: 5 minutes | Serves 4

1 cup cranberry juice cocktail

¼ cup agave nectar

2 cups frozen cherry berry blend

1. In a large bowl, add the agave nectar and cranberry juice cocktail and beat until well combined. 2. Place the cherry berry blend into an empty Ninja CREAMi pint container. 3. Top with cocktail mixture and stir to combine. 4. Cover the container with storage lid and freeze for 24 hours. 5. After 24 hours, remove the lid from container and arrange into the Outer Bowl of Ninja CREAMi. 6. Install the Creamerizer Paddle onto the lid of outer bowl. 7. Then rotate the lid clockwise to lock. 8. Press Power button to turn on the unit. 9. Then press Smoothie Bowl button. 10. When the program is completed, turn the Outer Bowl and release it from the machine. 11. Transfer the smoothie into serving bowls and serve immediately.

Chapter 6 Sorbet Recipes

Chapter 6 Sorbet Recipes

Coconut Lime Sorbet

Prep time: 5 minutes | Cook time: 30 minutes | Serves 5

1 can coconut cream
½ cup coconut water
¼ cup lime juice
½ tablespoon lime zest
¼ teaspoon coconut extract (optional)

1. Combine the coconut cream, coconut water, lime juice, lime zest, and coconut extract in a mixing bowl. Cover with plastic wrap and refrigerate for at least 1 hour, or until the flavors have melded. 2. Add the mixture to the Ninja CREAMi Pint container and freeze on a level surface in a cold freezer for a full 24 hours. 3. After 24 hours, remove the Pint from the freezer. Remove the lid. 4. Place the Ninja CREAMi Pint into the outer bowl. Place the outer bowl with the Pint in it into the ninja CREAMi machine and turn until the outer bowl locks into place. Push the SORBET button. During the SORBET function, the sorbet will mix together and become very creamy. This should take approximately 2 minutes. 5. Once the SORBET function has ended, turn the outer bowl and release it from the ninja CREAMi machine. 6. Your sorbet is ready to eat! Enjoy!

Cherry-berry Rosé Sorbet

Prep time: 5 minutes | Cook time: 10 minutes | Serves 3

2 cups frozen cherry-berry fruit blend
½ cup rosé wine, or as needed
¼ cup white sugar, or to taste
¼ medium lemon, juiced

1. Add all ingredients to a bowl and mix until the sugar dissolves. Place the mixture in the ninja CREAMi Pint container and freeze on a level surface in a cold freezer for a full 24 hours. 2. After 24 hours, remove the Pint from the freezer. Remove the lid. 3. Place the Ninja CREAMi Pint into the outer bowl. Place the outer bowl with the Pint in it into the ninja CREAMi machine and turn until the outer bowl locks into place. Push the SORBET button. During the SORBET function, the sorbet will mix together and become very creamy. This should take approximately 2 minutes. 4. Once the SORBET function has ended, turn the outer bowl and release it from the ninja CREAMi machine. 5. Your sorbet is ready to eat! Enjoy!

Celery Sorbet

Prep time: 5 minutes | Cook time: 5 minutes | Serves 3

½ cup white sugar
½ cup cold water
½ pound trimmed celery
Pinch of salt, or to taste
½ medium lime, juiced

1. In a saucepan over medium heat, combine the sugar and water until it just begins to boil. Remove the pan from the heat. While the other ingredients are being prepared, cool the simple syrup to room temperature. 2. The celery should be cut into tiny pieces. Combine the salt, lime juice, and the cooled simple syrup in a mixing bowl. Blend until completely smooth. 3. Fill a sieve with the mixture. Using a spoon, press the mixture through the strainer until all of the juice has been removed. Cover and refrigerate the juice for at least 1 hour or until completely cooled. 4. Put the cooled mixture into the ninja CREAMi Pint container and freeze on a level surface in a cold freezer for a full 24 hours. 5. After 24 hours, remove the Pint from the freezer. Remove the lid. 6. Place the Ninja CREAMi Pint into the outer bowl. Place the outer bowl with the Pint in it into the ninja CREAMi machine and turn until the outer bowl locks into place. Push the SORBET button. During the SORBET function, the sorbet will mix together and become very creamy. This should take approximately 2 minutes. 7. Once the SORBET function has ended, turn the outer bowl and release it from the ninja CREAMi machine. 8. Your sorbet is ready to eat! Enjoy!

Strawberry Sorbet

Prep time: 5 minutes | Cook time: 5 minutes | Serves 4
6 ounces daiquiri mix
2 ounces rum
½ cup frozen strawberries
½ cup simple syrup

1. In an empty Ninja CREAMi pint container, add all the ingredients and mix well. 2. Cover the container with storage lid and freeze for 24 hours. 3. After 24 hours, remove the lid from container and arrange into the Outer Bowl of Ninja CREAMi. 4. Install the Creamerizer Paddle onto the lid of Outer Bowl. 5. Then rotate the lid clockwise to lock. 6. Press Power button to turn on the unit. 7. Then press Sorbet button. 8. When the program is completed, turn the Outer Bowl and release it from the machine. 9. Transfer the sorbet into serving bowls and serve immediately.

Plum Sorbet

Prep time: 5 minutes | Cook time: 5 minutes | Serves 4

1 can plums

1. Place the plums into an empty Ninja CREAMi pint container. 2. Cover the container with storage lid and freeze for 24 hours. 3. After 24 hours, remove the lid from container and arrange into the Outer Bowl of Ninja CREAMi. 4. Install the Creamerizer Paddle onto the lid of Outer Bowl. 5. Then rotate the lid clockwise to lock. 6. Press Power button to turn on the unit. 7. Then press Sorbet button. 8. When the program is completed, turn the Outer Bowl and release it from the machine. 9. Transfer the sorbet into serving bowls and serve immediately.

Pineapple & Rum Sorbet

Prep time: 5 minutes | Cook time: 5 minutes | Serves 4

¾ cup piña colada mix
¼ cup rum
2 tablespoons granulated sugar
1½ cups frozen pineapple chunks

1. In a high-speed blender, add all the ingredients and pulse until smooth. 2. Transfer the mixture into an empty Ninja CREAMi pint container. 3. Cover the container with storage lid and freeze for 24 hours. 4. After 24 hours, remove the lid from container and arrange into the Outer Bowl of Ninja CREAMi. 5. Install the Creamerizer Paddle onto the lid of Outer Bowl. 6. Then rotate the lid clockwise to lock. 7. Press Power button to turn on the unit. 8. Then press Sorbet button. 9. When the program is completed, turn the Outer Bowl and release it from the machine. 10. Transfer the sorbet into serving bowls and serve immediately.

Peach Sorbet

Prep time: 5 minutes | Cook time: 5 minutes | Serves 4

1 cup passionfruit seltzer
3 tablespoons agave nectar
1 can peaches in heavy syrup, drained

1. In a bowl, add the seltzer and agave and beat until agave is dissolved. 2. Place the peaches into an empty Ninja CREAMi pint container and top with seltzer mixture. 3. Cover the container with storage lid and freeze for 24 hours. 4. After 24 hours, remove the lid from container and arrange into the Outer Bowl of Ninja CREAMi. 5. Install the Creamerizer Paddle onto the lid of Outer Bowl. 6. Then rotate the lid clockwise to lock. 7. Press Power button to turn on the unit. 8. Then press Sorbet button. 9. When the program is completed, turn the Outer Bowl and release it from the machine. 10. Transfer the sorbet into serving bowls and serve immediately.

Raspberry Lime Sorbet

Prep time: 5 minutes | Cook time: 5 minutes | Serves 4

2 cups fresh raspberries
5 ounces simple syrup
6 tablespoons fresh lime juice

1. In an empty Ninja CREAMi pint container, add all the ingredients and mix well. 2. Cover the container with the storage lid and freeze for 24 hours. 3. After 24 hours, remove the lid from container and arrange into the outer bowl of Ninja CREAMi. 4. Install the "Creamerizer Paddle" onto the lid of outer bowl. 5. Then rotate the lid clockwise to lock. 6. Press "Power" button to turn on the unit. 7. Then press "SORBET" button. 8. When the program is completed, turn the outer bowl and release it from the machine. 9. Transfer the sorbet into serving bowls and serve immediately.

Banana Sorbet

Prep time: 5 minutes | Cook time: 5 minutes | Serves 2

1 frozen banana
1 teaspoon cold water
2 teaspoons caramel sauce

1. Add the banana, water, and caramel sauce into the ninja CREAMi Pint container and freeze on a level surface in a cold freezer for a full 24 hours. 2. After 24 hours, remove the Pint from the freezer. Remove the lid. 3. Place the Ninja CREAMi Pint into the outer bowl. Place the outer bowl with the Pint in it into the ninja CREAMi machine and turn until the outer bowl locks into place. Push the SORBET button. During the SORBET function, the sorbet will mix together and become very creamy. This should take approximately 2 minutes. 4. Once the SORBET function has ended, turn the outer bowl and release it from the ninja CREAMi machine.

Raspberry Sorbet

Prep time: 5 minutes | Cook time: 5 minutes | Serves 4

3 cups fresh raspberries
⅓ cup water
⅓ cup sugar
¾ cup berry punch

1. In a high-speed blender, add all the ingredients and pulse until smooth. 2. Transfer the mixture into an empty Ninja CREAMi pint container. 3. Cover the container with storage lid and freeze for 24 hours. 4. After 24 hours, remove the lid from container and arrange into the Outer Bowl of Ninja CREAMi. 5. Install the Creamerizer Paddle onto the lid of Outer Bowl. 6. Then rotate the lid clockwise to lock. 7. Press Power button to turn on the unit. 8. Then press Sorbet button. 9. When the program is completed, turn the Outer Bowl and release it from the machine. 10. Transfer the sorbet into serving bowls and serve immediately.

Lemony Herb Sorbet

Prep time: 5 minutes | Cook time: 6 minutes | Serves 4

½ cup water	2 large fresh basil sprigs, stemmed
¼ cup granulated sugar	1 cup ice water
2 large fresh dill sprigs, stemmed	2 tablespoons fresh lemon juice

1. In a small saucepan, add sugar and water and over medium heat and cook for about five minutes or until the sugar is dissolved, stirring continuously. 2. Stir in the herb sprigs and remove from the heat. 3. Add the ice water and lemon juice and stir to combine. 4. Transfer the mixture into an empty Ninja CREAMi pint container. 5. Cover the container with storage lid and freeze for 24 hours. 6. After 24 hours, remove the lid from container and arrange into the Outer Bowl of Ninja CREAMi. 7. Install the Creamerizer Paddle onto the lid of Outer Bowl. 8. Then rotate the lid clockwise to lock. 9. Press Power button to turn on the unit. 10. Then press Sorbet button. 11. When the program is completed, turn the Outer Bowl and release it from the machine. 12. Transfer the sorbet into serving bowls and serve immediately.

Lime Beer Sorbet

Prep time: 5 minutes | Cook time: 5 minutes | Serves 4

¾ cup beer	½ cup fresh lime juice
⅔ cup water	¼ cup granulated sugar

1. In a high-speed blender, add all the ingredients and pulse until smooth. 2. Set aside for about 5 minutes. 3. Transfer the mixture into an empty Ninja CREAMi pint container. 4. Cover the container with the storage lid and freeze for 24 hours. 5. After 24 hours, remove the lid from container and arrange into the outer bowl of Ninja CREAMi. 6. Install the "Creamerizer Paddle" onto the lid of outer bowl. 7. Then rotate the lid clockwise to lock. 8. Press "Power" button to turn on the unit. 9. Then press "SORBET" button. 10. When the program is completed, turn the outer bowl and release it from the machine 11. Transfer the sorbet into serving bowls and serve immediately.

Mango Sorbet

Prep time: 5 minutes | Cook time: 5 minutes | Serves 4

4 cups mangoes, peeled, pitted and chopped	⅓-½ cup sugar
½ cup water	¼ cup fresh lime juice
	2 tablespoons Chamoy

1. In a high-speed blender, add mangoes and water and pulse until smooth. 2. Through a fine-mesh strainer, strain the mango puree into a large bowl. 3. Add the sugar, lime juice and chamoy and stir to combine. 4. Transfer the mixture into an empty Ninja CREAMi pint container. 5. Cover the container with storage lid and freeze for 24 hours. 6. After 24 hours, remove the lid from container and arrange into the Outer Bowl of Ninja CREAMi. 7. Install the Creamerizer Paddle onto the lid of Outer Bowl. 8. Then rotate the lid clockwise to lock. 9. Press Power button to turn on the unit. 10. Then press Sorbet button. 11. When the program is completed, turn the Outer Bowl and release it from the machine. 12. Transfer the sorbet into serving bowls and serve immediately.

Mango Chamoy Sorbet

Prep time: 5 minutes | Cook time: 5 minutes | Serves 4

4 cups mangoes, peeled, pitted and chopped	⅓-½ cup sugar
½ cup water	¼ cup fresh lime juice
	2 tablespoons chamoy

1. In a high-speed blender, add mangoes and water and pulse until smooth. 2. Through a fine-mesh strainer, strain the mango puree into a large bowl. 3. Add the sugar, lime juice and chamoy and stir to combine. 4. Transfer the mixture into an empty Ninja CREAMi pint container. 5. Cover the container with the storage lid and freeze for 24 hours. 6. After 24 hours, remove the lid from container and arrange into the outer bowl of Ninja CREAMi. 7. Install the "Creamerizer Paddle" onto the lid of outer bowl. 8. Then rotate the lid clockwise to lock. 9. Press "Power" button to turn on the unit. 10. Then press "SORBET" button. 11. When the program is completed, turn the outer bowl and release it from the machine. 12. Transfer the sorbet into serving bowls and serve immediately.

Avocado Lime Sorbet

Prep time: 5 minutes | Cook time: 5 minutes | Serves 4

¾ cup water	1 large ripe avocado, peeled, pitted and chopped
2 tablespoons light corn syrup	3 ounces fresh lime juice
Pinch of sea salt	
⅔ cup granulated sugar	

1. In a medium saucepan, add water, corn syrup and salt and beat until well combined. 2. Place the saucepan over medium heat. 3. Slowly add the sugar, continuously beating until well combined and bring to a boil. 4. Remove the saucepan from heat and set aside to cool completely. 5. In a high-speed blender, add the sugar mixture, avocado and lime juice and pulse until smooth. 6. Transfer the mixture into an empty Ninja CREAMi pint container. 7. Cover the container with the storage lid and freeze for 24 hours. 8. After 24 hours, remove the lid from container and arrange into the outer bowl of Ninja CREAMi. 9. Install the "Creamerizer Paddle" onto the lid of outer bowl. 10. Then rotate the lid clockwise to lock. 11. Press "Power" button to turn on the unit. 12. Then press "SORBET" button. 13. When the program is completed, turn the outer bowl and release it from the machine. 14. Transfer the sorbet into serving bowls and serve immediately.

Pear Sorbet

Prep time: 5 minutes | Cook time: 5 minutes | Serves 4

1 can pears in light syrup

1. Place the pear pieces into an empty Ninja CREAMi to the MAX FILL line. 2. Cover the orange pieces with syrup from the can. 3. Cover the container with the storage lid and freeze for 24 hours. 4. After 24 hours, remove the lid from container and arrange into the outer bowl of Ninja CREAMi. 5. Install the "Creamerizer Paddle" onto the lid of outer bowl. 6. Then rotate the lid clockwise to lock. 7. Press "Power" button to turn on the unit. 8. Then press "SORBET" button. 9. When the program is completed, turn the outer bowl and release it from the machine. 10. Transfer the sorbet into serving bowls and serve immediately.

Acai & Fruit Sorbet

Prep time: 5 minutes | Cook time: 5 minutes | Serves 4

1 packet frozen acai	¼ cup granulated sugar
½ cup blackberries	1 cup water
½ cup banana, peeled and sliced	

1. In a high-speed blender, add all the ingredients and pulse until smooth. 2. Transfer the mixture into an empty Ninja CREAMi pint container. 3. Cover the container with storage lid and freeze for 24 hours. 4. After 24 hours, remove the lid from container and arrange into the Outer Bowl of Ninja CREAMi. 5. Install the Creamerizer Paddle onto the lid of Outer Bowl. 6. Then rotate the lid clockwise to lock. 7. Press Power button to turn on the unit. 8. Then press Sorbet button. 9. When the program is completed, turn the Outer Bowl and release it from the machine. 10. Transfer the sorbet into serving bowls and serve immediately.

Cherry Sorbet

Prep time: 5 minutes | Cook time: 5 minutes | Serves 4

1½ cups cola	¼ cup water
⅓ cup maraschino cherries	1 tablespoon fresh lime juice
⅓ cup spiced rum	

1. In a high-speed blender, add all the ingredients and pulse until smooth. 2. Transfer the mixture into an empty Ninja CREAMi pint container. 3. Cover the container with the storage lid and freeze for 24 hours. 4. After 24 hours, remove the lid from container and arrange into the outer bowl of Ninja CREAMi. 5. Install the "Creamerizer Paddle" onto the lid of outer bowl. 6. Then rotate the lid clockwise to lock. 7. Press "Power" button to turn on the unit. 8. Then press "SORBET" button. 9. When the program is completed, turn the outer bowl and release it from the machine. 10. Transfer the sorbet into serving bowls and serve immediately.

Pomegranate Sorbet Smile

Prep time: 5 minutes | Cook time: 45 minutes | Serves 4

1 pomegranate	squeezed lemon juice
½ cup white sugar	1½ egg whites
1½ tablespoons freshly	1 cup heavy whipping cream

1. With a knife, score the pomegranate rinds lengthwise and crosswise. With the knife, carefully break open the fruit. Using the scored lines as a guide, cut the flesh into quarters with your hands. To release the seeds, hold each quarter over a big basin and beat it forcefully with a wooden spoon. 2. To release some liquid, crush the seeds in the basin with a potato masher. Continue mashing to release additional liquid after adding the sugar and lemon juice. 3. In a glass, metal, or ceramic bowl, whisk the egg whites until firm peaks form. Mash in the pomegranate mixture. 4. In a cold glass or metal bowl, beat the cream until thick. To get the correct consistency, mash it into the pomegranate mixture, popping the seeds as needed. 5. Put the mixture into the ninja CREAMi Pint container and freeze on a level surface in a cold freezer for a full 24 hours. 6. After 24 hours, remove the Pint from the freezer. Remove the lid. 7. Place the Ninja CREAMi Pint into the outer bowl. Place the outer bowl with the Pint in it into the ninja CREAMi machine and turn until the outer bowl locks into place. Push the SORBET button. During the SORBET function, the sorbet will mix together and become very creamy. This should take approximately 2 minutes. 8. Once the SORBET function has ended, turn the outer bowl and release it from the ninja CREAMi machine. 9. Your sorbet is ready to eat! Enjoy!

Italian Ice Sorbet

Prep time: 5 minutes | Cook time: 5 minutes | Serves 1

12 ounces lemonade	is quite tart, use 6 ounces of
Sugar or your preferred	lemonade and 6 ounces of
sweetener to taste (optional)	water instead of 12 ounces of
If the lemonade you're using	lemonade

1. Pour the lemonade (or lemonade and water mixture) into a ninja CREAMi Pint container and freeze on a level surface in a cold freezer for a full 24 hours. 2. After 24 hours, remove the Pint from the freezer. Remove the lid. 3. Place the Ninja CREAMi Pint into the outer bowl. Place the outer bowl with the Pint in it into the ninja CREAMi machine and turn until the outer bowl locks into place. Push the SORBET button. During the SORBET function, the sorbet will mix together and become very creamy. This should take approximately 2 minutes. 4. Once the SORBET function has ended, turn the outer bowl and release it from the ninja CREAMi machine.

Strawberry & Beet Sorbet

Prep time: 5 minutes | Cook time: 5 minutes | Serves 4

2⅔ cups strawberries, hulled and quartered
⅓ cup cooked beets, quartered
⅓ cup granulated sugar
⅓ cup orange juice

1. In a high-speed blender, add mangoes and beets and pulse until smooth. 2. Through a fine-mesh strainer, strain the mango puree into a large bowl. 3. Add the sugar and orange juice and and stir to combine. 4. Transfer the mixture into an empty Ninja CREAMi pint container. 5. Cover the container with the storage lid and freeze for 24 hours. 6. After 24 hours, remove the lid from container and arrange into the outer bowl of Ninja CREAMi. 7. Install the "Creamerizer Paddle" onto the lid of outer bowl. 8. Then rotate the lid clockwise to lock. 9. Press "Power" button to turn on the unit. 10. Then press "SORBET" button. 11. When the program is completed, turn the outer bowl and release it from the machine. 12. Transfer the sorbet into serving bowls and serve immediately.

Strawberries & Champagne Sorbet

Prep time: 5 minutes | Cook time: 15 minutes | Serves 3

1 packet strawberry-flavored gelatin (such as Jell-O)
¾ cup boiling water
½ cup light corn syrup
3 fluid ounces champagne
1 egg whites, slightly beaten

1. Dissolve the gelatin in boiling water in a bowl. Beat in the corn syrup, champagne, and egg whites. 2. Put the mixture into the ninja CREAMi Pint container and freeze on a level surface in a cold freezer for a full 24 hours. 3. After 24 hours, remove the Pint from the freezer. Remove the lid. 4. Place the Ninja CREAMi Pint into the outer bowl. Place the outer bowl with the Pint in it into the ninja CREAMi machine and turn until the outer bowl locks into place. Push the SORBET button. During the SORBET function, the sorbet will mix together and become very creamy. This should take approximately 2 minutes. 5. Once the SORBET function has ended, turn the outer bowl and release it from the ninja CREAMi machine. 6. Your sorbet is ready to eat! Enjoy!

Blueberry Lemon Sorbet

Prep time: 5 minutes | Cook time: 5 minutes | Serves 1

1 tablespoon cream cheese
¼ cup milk
1½ cups lemonade
⅓ cup blueberries (fresh or frozen)

1. In a medium mixing bowl, whisk together the softened cream cheese and the milk. Make an effort to integrate the two as much as possible. Some little bits of cream cheese may remain, but that's fine as long as they're small. 2. Add the lemonade and stir thoroughly. 3. Pour the mixture into a ninja CREAMi Pint container, add the blueberries and freeze on a level surface in a cold freezer for a full 24 hours. 4. After 24 hours, remove the Pint from the freezer. Remove the lid. 5. Place the Ninja CREAMi Pint into the outer bowl. Place the outer bowl with the Pint in it into the ninja CREAMi machine and turn until the outer bowl locks into place. Push the SORBET button. During the SORBET function, the sorbet will mix together and become very creamy. This should take approximately 2 minutes. 6. Once the SORBET function has ended, turn the outer bowl and release it from the ninja CREAMi machine. 7. Your sorbet is ready to eat! Enjoy! 8. Place the outer bowl with the Pint back into the ninja CREAMi machine and lock it into place if the sorbet isn't quite creamy enough. Select the RE-SPIN option. Remove the outer bowl from the Ninja CREAMi after the RE-SPIN cycle is complete.

Grape Sorbet

Prep time: 5 minutes | Cook time: 5 minutes | Serves 4

¾ cup frozen grape juice concentrate
1½ cups water
1 tablespoon fresh lemon juice

1. In a bowl, add all the ingredients and beat until well combined. 2. Transfer the mixture into an empty Ninja CREAMi pint container. 3. Cover the container with storage lid and freeze for 24 hours. 4. After 24 hours, remove the lid from container and arrange into the Outer Bowl of Ninja CREAMi. 5. Install the Creamerizer Paddle onto the lid of Outer Bowl. 6. Then rotate the lid clockwise to lock. 7. Press Power button to turn on the unit. 8. Then press Sorbet button. 9. When the program is completed, turn the Outer Bowl and release it from the machine. 10. Transfer the sorbet into serving bowls and serve immediately.

Blueberry & Pomegranate Sorbet

Prep time: 5 minutes | Cook time: 5 minutes | Serves 4

1 can blueberries in light syrup
½ cup pomegranate juice

1. In an empty Ninja CREAMi pint container, place the blueberries and top with syrup. 2. Add in the pomegranate juice and stir to combine. 3. Cover the container with the storage lid and freeze for 24 hours. 4. After 24 hours, remove the lid from container and arrange into the outer bowl of Ninja CREAMi. 5. Install the "Creamerizer Paddle" onto the lid of outer bowl. 6. Then rotate the lid clockwise to lock 7. Press "Power" button to turn on the unit. 8. Then press "SORBET" button. 9. When the program is completed, turn the outer bowl and release it from the machine. 10. Transfer the sorbet into serving bowls and serve immediately.

Mojito Sorbet

Prep time: 5 minutes | Cook time: 5 minutes | Serves 8

- ½ cup water
- ½ cup white sugar
- ¼ cup mint leaves, packed
- 1 teaspoon grated lime zest
- ½ cup freshly squeezed lime juice
- ¾ cup citrus-flavored sparkling water
- 1 tablespoon rum (optional)

1. Add all ingredients to a bowl and mix until the sugar is dissolved. Pour into the ninja CREAMi Pint container and freeze on a level surface in a cold freezer for a full 24 hours. 2. After 24 hours, remove the Pint from the freezer. Remove the lid. 3. Place the Ninja CREAMi Pint into the outer bowl. Place the outer bowl with the Pint in it into the ninja CREAMi machine and turn until the outer bowl locks into place. Push the SORBET button. During the SORBET function, the sorbet will mix together and become very creamy. This should take approximately 2 minutes. 4. Once the SORBET function has ended, turn the outer bowl and release it from the ninja CREAMi machine. 5. Your sorbet is ready to eat! Enjoy!

Mango Margarita Sorbet

Prep time: 5 minutes | Cook time: 5 minutes | Serves 4

- ¾ cup margarita mix
- 3 tablespoons gold tequila
- 2 tablespoons fresh lime juice
- 1 tablespoon agave nectar
- ¼ teaspoon cayenne pepper
- ¼ teaspoon salt
- 1 can mango chunks

1. In a bowl, add all ingredients except for mango chunks and beat until well combined. 2. Add mango chunks and toss to coat. 3. Transfer the mixture into an empty Ninja CREAMi pint container. 4. Cover the container with the storage lid and freeze for 24 hours. 5. After 24 hours, remove the lid from container and arrange into the outer bowl of Ninja CREAMi. 6. Install the "Creamerizer Paddle" onto the lid of outer bowl. 7. Then rotate the lid clockwise to lock. 8. Press "Power" button to turn on the unit. 9. Then press "SORBET" button. 10. When the program is completed, turn the outer bowl and release it from the machine. 11. Transfer the sorbet into serving bowls and serve immediately.

Kiwi & Strawberry Sorbet

Prep time: 5 minutes | Cook time: 5 minutes | Serves 4

- 2 cups frozen sliced strawberries
- 4 kiwis, peeled and cut into 1-inch pieces
- ¼ cup agave nectar
- ¼ cup water

1. In a high-speed blender, add all the ingredients and pulse until smooth. 2. Transfer the mixture into an empty Ninja CREAMi pint container. 3. Cover the container with storage lid and freeze for 24 hours. 4. After 24 hours, remove the lid from container and arrange into the Outer Bowl of Ninja CREAMi. 5. Install the Creamerizer Paddle onto the lid of Outer Bowl. 6. Then rotate the lid clockwise to lock. 7. Press Power button to turn on the unit. 8. Then press Sorbet button. 9. When the program is completed, turn the Outer Bowl and release it from the machine. 10. Transfer the sorbet into serving bowls and serve immediately.

Mixed Berries Sorbet

Prep time: 5 minutes | Cook time: 5 minutes | Serves 4

- 1 cup blueberries
- 1 cup raspberries
- 1 cup strawberries, hulled and quartered

1. In an empty Ninja CREAMi pint container, place the berries and with a potato masher, mash until well combined. 2. Cover the container with storage lid and freeze for 24 hours. 3. After 24 hours, remove the lid from container and arrange into the outer bowl of Ninja CREAMi. 4. Install the Creamerizer Paddle onto the lid of Outer Bowl. 5. Then rotate the lid clockwise to lock. 6. Press Power button to turn on the unit. 7. Then press Sorbet button. 8. When the program is completed, turn the Outer Bowl and release it from the machine. 9. Transfer the sorbet into serving bowls and serve immediately.

Pineapple Sorbet

Prep time: 5 minutes | Cook time: 5 minutes | Serves 1

12 ounces canned pineapple

1. Pour the pineapple, with the liquid from the can, into a ninja CREAMi Pint container and freeze on a level surface in a cold freezer for a full 24 hours. 2. After 24 hours, remove the Pint from the freezer. Remove the lid. 3. Place the Ninja CREAMi Pint into the outer bowl. Place the outer bowl with the Pint in it into the ninja CREAMi machine and turn until the outer bowl locks into place. Push the SORBET button. During the SORBET function, the sorbet will mix together and become very creamy. This should take approximately 2 minutes. 4. Once the SORBET function has ended, turn the outer bowl and release it from the ninja CREAMi machine. 5. Your sorbet is ready to eat! Enjoy!

Chapter 7 Milkshake Recipes

Chapter 7 Milkshake Recipes

Healthy Strawberry Shake

Prep time: 5 minutes | Cook time: 10 minutes | Serves 1

1 cup milk
1 tablespoon honey
½ teaspoon vanilla extract
½ cup frozen strawberries

1. Add the milk, honey, vanilla extract, and strawberries into an empty CREAMi Pint. 2. Place Pint in outer bowl, install Creamerizer Paddle onto outer bowl lid and lock the lid assembly on the outer bowl. Place the bowl assembly on the motor base and crank the lever to elevate and secure the platform in place. 3. Select MILKSHAKE. 4. Remove the milkshake from the Pint after the processing is finished.

Chocolate Cherry Milkshake

Prep time: 5 minutes | Cook time: 4 minutes | Serves 4

1½ cups chocolate ice cream
½ cup canned cherries in syrup, drained
¼ cup whole milk

1. In an empty Ninja CREAMi pint container, place ice cream followed by cherries and milk. 2. Arrange the container into the Outer Bowl of Ninja CREAMi. 3. Install the Creamerizer Paddle onto the lid of Outer Bowl. 4. Then rotate the lid clockwise to lock. 5. Press Power button to turn on the unit. 6. Then press Milkshake button. 7. When the program is completed, turn the Outer Bowl and release it from the machine. 8. Transfer the shake into serving glasses and serve immediately.

Lemon Meringue Pie Milkshake

Prep time: 5 minutes | Cook time: 5 minutes | Serves 1

1 cup vanilla ice cream
4 tablespoons store-bought lemon curd, divided
4 tablespoons marshmallow topping, divided
½ cup Graham Crackers, broken, divided

1. Place the ice cream in an empty CREAMi Pint. 2. Use a spoon to create a 1½-inch wide hole that reaches the bottom of the Pint. Add the remaining ingredients to the hole. 3. Place Pint in outer bowl, install Creamerizer Paddle onto outer bowl lid and lock the lid assembly on the outer bowl. Place the bowl assembly on the motor base and crank the lever to elevate and secure the platform in place. 4. Select the MILKSHAKE option. 5. Remove the milkshake from the Pint after the processing is finished.

Chocolate-hazelnut Milkshake

Prep time: 5 minutes | Cook time: 3 minutes | Serves 4

2 tablespoons granulated sugar
2 tablespoons unsweetened cocoa powder
½ cup whole milk
1 cup hazelnut-flavored coffee creamer

1. In a large bowl, whisk together the sugar, cocoa powder, milk, and coffee creamer until the sugar is fully dissolved. 2. Pour the base into a clean CREAMi Pint. Place the storage lid on the container and freeze for 24 hours. 3. Remove the pint from the freezer and take off the lid. Place the pint in the outer bowl of your Ninja CREAMi, install the Creamerizer Paddle in the outer bowl lid, and lock the lid assembly onto the outer bowl. Place the bowl assembly on the motor base, and twist the handle to the right to raise the platform and lock it in place. Select the Milkshake function. 4. Once the machine has finished processing, remove the milkshake from the pint. Serve immediately.

Boozy Amaretto Cookie Milkshake

Prep time: 5 minutes | Cook time: 3 minutes | Serves 4

1 cup whole milk
½ cup amaretto-flavored coffee creamer
¼ cup amaretto liqueur
1 tablespoon agave nectar
¼ cup chopped chocolate chip cookies

1. In a clean CREAMi Pint, combine the milk, coffee creamer, amaretto liqueur, and agave. Stir well. Place the storage lid on the container and freeze for 24 hours. 2. Remove the pint from the freezer and take off the lid. Add the chocolate chip cookies to the top of the pint. Place the pint in the outer bowl of your Ninja CREAMi, install the Creamerizer Paddle in the outer bowl lid, and lock the lid assembly onto the outer bowl. Place the bowl assembly on the motor base, and twist the handle to the right to raise the platform and lock it in place. Select the Milkshake function. 3. Once the machine has finished processing, remove the lid. With a spoon, create a 1½-inch-wide hole that reaches the bottom of the pint. During this process, it is okay if your treat reaches above the Max Fill line. Add the chopped cookies to the hole in the pint, replace the lid, and select Milkshake. Serve immediately.

Chocolate-peanut Butter Milkshake

Prep time: 5 minutes | Cook time: 3 minutes | Serves 2

1½ cups chocolate ice cream
½ cup whole milk
¼ cup mini peanut butter cups

1. Combine the chocolate ice cream and milk in a clean CREAMi Pint. 2. Use a spoon to create a 1½-inch-wide hole that goes all the way to the bottom of the pint. Pour the mini peanut butter cups into the hole. 3. Place the pint in the outer bowl of your Ninja CREAMi, install the Creamerizer Paddle in the outer bowl lid, and lock the lid assembly onto the outer bowl. Place the bowl assembly on the motor base, and twist the handle to the right to raise the platform and lock it in place. Select the Milkshake function. 4. Once the machine has finished processing, remove the milkshake from the pint. Serve immediately.

Cacao Mint Milkshake

Prep time: 5 minutes | Cook time: 3 minutes | Serves 2

1½ cups vanilla ice cream
½ cup canned full-fat coconut milk
1 teaspoon matcha powder
¼ cup cacao nibs
1 teaspoon peppermint extract

1. In an empty Ninja CREAMi pint container, place ice cream followed by coconut milk, matcha powder, cacao nibs and peppermint extract. 2. Arrange the container into the Outer Bowl of Ninja CREAMi. 3. Install the Creamerizer Paddle onto the lid of Outer Bowl. 4. Then rotate the lid clockwise to lock. 5. Press Power button to turn on the unit. 6. Then press Milkshake button. 7. When the program is completed, turn the Outer Bowl and release it from the machine. 8. Transfer the shake into serving glasses and serve immediately.

Amaretto Cookies Milkshake

Prep time: 5 minutes | Cook time: 3 minutes | Serves 2

1 cup whole milk
½ cup amaretto-flavored coffee creamer
¼ cup amaretto liqueur
1 tablespoon agave nectar
¼ cup chocolate chip cookies, chopped

1. In an empty Ninja CREAMi pint container, place all ingredients except for cookies and stir to combine. 2. Cover the container with the storage lid and freeze for 24 hours. 3. After 24 hours, remove the lid from container and arrange into the outer bowl of Ninja CREAMi. 4. Install the "Creamerizer Paddle" onto the lid of outer bowl. 5. Then rotate the lid clockwise to lock. 6. Press "Power" button to turn on the unit. 7. Then press "MILKSHAKE" button. 8. When the program is completed, with a spoon, create a 1½-inch wide hole in the center that reaches the bottom of the pint container. 9. Add the chopped cookies into the hole and press "MIX-IN" button. 10. When the program is completed, turn the outer bowl and release it from the machine. 11. Transfer the shake into serving glasses and serve immediately.

Frozen Mudslide

Prep time: 5 minutes | Cook time: 3 minutes | Serves 2

2 cups ice cubes
½ cup store-bought vanilla ice cream
6 tablespoons espresso vodka
6 tablespoons coffee-flavored liqueur
6 tablespoons Irish cream-flavored liqueur

1. Combine the ice, ice cream, vodka, and liqueurs in a blender. Blend on high until smooth. 2. Pour the base into a clean CREAMi Pint. Place the storage lid on the container and freeze for 24 hours. 3. Remove the pint from the freezer and take off the lid. Place the pint in the outer bowl of your Ninja CREAMi, install the Creamerizer Paddle in the outer bowl lid, and lock the lid assembly onto the outer bowl. Place the bowl assembly on the motor base, and twist the handle to the right to raise the platform and lock it in place. Select the Milkshake function. 4. Once the machine has finished processing, remove the milkshake from the pint. Serve immediately.

Orange Milkshake

Prep time: 5 minutes | Cook time: 5 minutes | Serves 1

1 cup orange juice
2 scoops vanilla ice cream
½ cup milk
2 teaspoons white sugar

1. Place orange juice, ice cream, milk, and sugar in an empty CREAMi Pint. 2. Place Pint in outer bowl, install Creamerizer Paddle onto outer bowl lid and lock the lid assembly on the outer bowl. Place the bowl assembly on the motor base and crank the lever to elevate and secure the platform in place. 3. Select MILKSHAKE. 4. Remove the milkshake from the Pint after the processing is finished.

Lime Sherbet Milkshake

Prep time: 5 minutes | Cook time: 3 minutes | Serves 1

1½ cups rainbow sherbet
½ cup lime seltzer

1. In an empty Ninja CREAMi pint container, place sherbet and top with lime seltzer. 2. Arrange the container into the outer bowl of Ninja CREAMi. 3. Install the "Creamerizer Paddle" onto the lid of outer bowl. 4. Then rotate the lid clockwise to lock. 5. Press "Power" button to turn on the unit. 6. Then press "MILKSHAKE" button. 7. When the program is completed, turn the outer bowl and release it from the machine. 8. Transfer the shake into a serving glass and serve immediately.

Chocolate Liqueur Milkshake

Prep time: 5 minutes | Cook time: 3 minutes | Serves 2

2 cups vanilla ice cream
⅓ cup chocolate liqueur
⅓ cup whole milk

1. In an empty Ninja CREAMi pint container, place ice cream, followed by chocolate liqueur and milk. 2. Arrange the container into the outer bowl of Ninja CREAMi. 3. Install the "Creamerizer Paddle" onto the lid of outer bowl. 4. Then rotate the lid clockwise to lock. 5. Press "Power" button to turn on the unit. 6. Then press "MILKSHAKE" button. 7. When the program is completed, turn the outer bowl and release it from the machine. 8. Transfer the shake into serving glasses and serve immediately.

Caramel Cone Milkshake

Prep time: 5 minutes | Cook time: 3 minutes | Serves 4

1½ cups vanilla ice cream
½ cup whole milk
3 tablespoons caramel sauce
1 waffle cone, crushed or finely chopped

1. Combine the vanilla ice cream, milk, and caramel sauce in a clean CREAMi Pint. 2. With a spoon, create a 1½-inch-wide hole that reaches the bottom of the pint. During this process, it is okay if your treat reaches above the Max Fill line. Add the crushed waffle cone to the hole in the pint. 3. Place the pint in the outer bowl of your Ninja CREAMi, install the Creamerizer Paddle in the outer bowl lid, and lock the lid assembly onto the outer bowl. Place the bowl assembly on the motor base, and twist the handle to the right to raise the platform and lock it in place. Select the Milkshake function. 4. Once the machine has finished processing, remove the milkshake from the pint. Serve immediately.

Dairy-free Strawberry Milkshake

Prep time: 5 minutes | Cook time: 3 minutes | Serves 2

1½ cups Coconut-Vanilla Ice Cream
½ cup oat milk
3 fresh strawberries

1. Combine the ice cream, oat milk, and strawberries in a clean CREAMi Pint. 2. Place the pint in the outer bowl of your Ninja CREAMi, install the Creamerizer Paddle in the outer bowl lid, and lock the lid assembly onto the outer bowl. Place the bowl assembly on the motor base, and twist the handle to the right to raise the platform and lock it in place. Select the Milkshake function. 3. Once the machine has finished processing, remove the milkshake from the pint. Serve immediately.

Peanut Butter Brownie Milkshake

Prep time: 5 minutes | Cook time: 5 minutes | Serves 2

½ cup chocolate ice cream
½ cup whole milk
2 tablespoons peanut butter, for mix-in
1¼ cups brownies, chopped into bite-sized pieces, for mix-in

1. Place the ice cream in an empty CREAMi Pint. 2. Use a spoon to create a 1½-inch wide hole that reaches the bottom of the Pint. Add the remaining ingredients to the hole. 3. Place Pint in outer bowl, install Creamerizer Paddle onto outer bowl lid and lock the lid assembly on the outer bowl. Place the bowl assembly on the motor base and crank the lever to elevate and secure the platform in place. 4. Select MILKSHAKE. 5. Remove the milkshake from the Pint after the processing is finished.

Vanilla Milkshake

Prep time: 5 minutes | Cook time: 3 minutes | Serves 2

2 cups French vanilla coffee creamer
1 tablespoon agave nectar
2 ounces vodka
1 tablespoon rainbow sprinkles

1. In an empty Ninja CREAMi pint container, place all ingredients and mix well. 2. Cover the container with storage lid and freeze for 24 hours. 3. After 24 hours, remove the lid from container and arrange into the Outer Bowl of Ninja CREAMi. 4. Install the Creamerizer Paddle onto the lid of Outer Bowl. 5. Then rotate the lid clockwise to lock. 6. Press Power button to turn on the unit. 7. Then press Milkshake button. 8. When the program is completed, turn the Outer Bowl and release it from the machine. 9. Transfer the shake into serving glasses and serve immediately.

Peanut Butter And Jelly Milkshake

Prep time: 5 minutes | Cook time: 5 minutes | Serves 2

3 tablespoons peanut butter
3 tablespoons grape jelly
1 cup milk
5 ice cubes
½ teaspoon vanilla extract

1. Add the milk, peanut butter, ice cubes, vanilla extract, and grape jelly into an empty CREAMi Pint. 2. Place the Pint in the outer bowl, install the Creamerizer Paddle onto the outer bowl lid and lock the lid assembly on the outer bowl. Place the bowl assembly on the motor base and crank the lever to elevate and secure the platform in place. 3. Choose the MILKSHAKE option. 4. Remove the milkshake from the Pint after the processing is finished.

Chocolate Yogurt Milkshake

Prep time: 5 minutes | Cook time: 3 minutes | Serves 2

1 cup frozen chocolate yogurt	powder
1 scoop chocolate whey protein	1 cup whole milk

1. In an empty Ninja CREAMi pint container, place yogurt followed by protein powder and milk. 2. Arrange the container into the Outer Bowl of Ninja CREAMi. 3. Install the Creamerizer Paddle onto the lid of Outer Bowl. 4. Then rotate the lid clockwise to lock. 5. Press Power button to turn on the unit. 6. Then press Milkshake button. 7. When the program is completed, turn the Outer Bowl and release it from the machine. 8. Transfer the shake into serving glasses and serve immediately.

Sugar Cookie Milkshake

Prep time: 8 minutes | Cook time: 5 minutes | Serves 1

½ cup vanilla ice cream	3 small sugar cookies, crushed
½ cup oat milk	2 tablespoons sprinkles

1. In an empty Ninja CREAMi pint container, place the ice cream. 2. With a spoon, create a 1½-inch wide hole in the center that reaches the bottom of the pint container. 3. Add the remaining ingredients into the hole. 4. Arrange the container into the outer bowl of Ninja CREAMi. 5. Install the "Creamerizer Paddle" onto the lid of outer bowl. 6. Then rotate the lid clockwise to lock. 7. Press "Power" button to turn on the unit. 8. Then press "MILKSHAKE" button. 9. When the program is completed, turn the outer bowl and release it from the machine. 10. Transfer the shake into a serving glass and serve immediately.

Avocado Milkshake

Prep time: 5 minutes | Cook time: 5 minutes | Serves 2

1 cup coconut ice cream	2 tablespoons agave nectar
1 small ripe avocado, peeled, pitted and chopped	1 teaspoon vanilla extract
	Pinch of salt
1 teaspoon fresh lemon juice	½ cup oat milk

1. In an empty Ninja CREAMi pint container, place ice cream, followed by remaining ingredients. 2. Arrange the container into the outer bowl of Ninja CREAMi. 3. Install the "Creamerizer Paddle" onto the lid of outer bowl. 4. Then rotate the lid clockwise to lock. 5. Press "Power" button to turn on the unit. 6. Then press "MILKSHAKE" button. 7. When the program is completed, turn the outer bowl and release it from the machine. 8. Transfer the shake into serving glasses and serve immediately.

Marshmallow Milkshake

Prep time: 5 minutes | Cook time: 3 minutes | Serves 2

1½ cups vanilla ice cream	½ cup marshmallow cereal
½ cup oat milk	

1. In an empty Ninja CREAMi pint container, place ice cream followed by oat milk and marshmallow cereal. 2. Arrange the container into the Outer Bowl of Ninja CREAMi. 3. Install the Creamerizer Paddle onto the lid of Outer Bowl. 4. Then rotate the lid clockwise to lock. 5. Press Power button to turn on the unit. 6. Then press Milkshake button. 7. When the program is completed, turn the Outer Bowl and release it from the machine. 8. Transfer the shake into serving glasses and serve immediately.

Cacao Matcha Milkshake

Prep time: 5 minutes | Cook time: 3 minutes | Serves 2

1½ cups vanilla ice cream	¼ cup cacao nibs
½ cup canned full-fat coconut milk	¾ teaspoon peppermint extract
1 teaspoon matcha powder	¼ teaspoon vanilla extract

1. In an empty Ninja CREAMi pint container, place ice cream, followed by coconut milk, matcha powder, cacao nibs and peppermint extract. 2. Arrange the container into the outer bowl of Ninja CREAMi. 3. Install the "Creamerizer Paddle" onto the lid of outer bowl. 4. Then rotate the lid clockwise to lock. 5. Press "Power" button to turn on the unit. 6. Then press "MILKSHAKE" button. 7. When the program is completed, turn the outer bowl and release it from the machine. 8. Transfer the shake into serving glasses and serve immediately.

Cashew Butter Milkshake

Prep time: 5 minutes | Cook time: 3 minutes | Serves 2

1½ cups vanilla ice cream	¼ cup cashew butter
½ cup canned cashew milk	

1. In an empty Ninja CREAMi pint container, place the ice cream. 2. With a spoon, create a 1½-inch wide hole in the center that reaches the bottom of the pint container. 3. Add the remaining ingredients into the hole. 4. Arrange the container into the Outer Bowl of Ninja CREAMi. 5. Install the Creamerizer Paddle onto the lid of Outer Bowl. 6. Then rotate the lid clockwise to lock. 7. Press Power button to turn on the unit. 8. Then press Milkshake button. 9. When the program is completed, turn the Outer Bowl and release it from the machine. 10. Transfer the shake into serving glasses and serve immediately.

Pecan Milkshake

Prep time: 5 minutes | Cook time: 3 minutes | Serves 2

1½ cups vanilla ice cream	¼ cup pecans, chopped
½ cup unsweetened soy milk	1 teaspoon ground cinnamon
2 tablespoons maple syrup	Pinch of salt

1. In an empty Ninja CREAMi pint container, place ice cream followed by soy milk, maple syrup, pecans, cinnamon and salt. 2. Arrange the container into the Outer Bowl of Ninja CREAMi. 3. Install the Creamerizer Paddle onto the lid of Outer Bowl. 4. Then rotate the lid clockwise to lock. 5. Press Power button to turn on the unit. 6. Then press Milkshake button. 7. When the program is completed, turn the Outer Bowl and release it from the machine. 8. Transfer the shake into serving glasses and serve immediately.

Lite Peanut Butter Ice Cream

Prep time: 5 minutes | Cook time: 3 minutes | Serves 4

1¾ cups fat-free (skim) milk	3 tablespoons smooth peanut butter
¼ cup stevia–cane sugar blend	
1 teaspoon vanilla extract	

1. In a medium bowl, whisk together the milk, stevia blend, vanilla extract, and peanut butter until the mixture is smooth and the stevia is fully dissolved. Let the mixture sit for about 5 minutes, until any foam subsides. If the stevia is still not dissolved, whisk again. 2. Pour the base into a clean CREAMi Pint. Place the storage lid on the container and freeze for 24 hours. 3. Remove the pint from the freezer and take off the lid. Place the pint in the outer bowl of your Ninja CREAMi, install the Creamerizer Paddle in the outer bowl lid, and lock the lid assembly onto the outer bowl. Place the bowl assembly on the motor base, and twist the handle to the right to raise the platform and lock it in place. Select the Lite Ice Cream function. 4. Once the machine has finished processing, remove the ice cream from the pint. Serve immediately.

Dulce De Leche Milkshake

Prep time: 5 minutes | Cook time: 5 minutes | Serves 2

1 cup vanilla or coffee ice cream	2 tablespoons sweetened condensed milk
½ cup milk	¼ teaspoon salt

1. Place all ingredients into an empty CREAMi Pint. 2. Place Pint in outer bowl, install Creamerizer Paddle onto outer bowl lid and lock the lid assembly on the outer bowl. Place the bowl assembly on the motor base and crank the lever to elevate and secure the platform in place. 3. Choose the MILKSHAKE option. 4. Remove the milkshake from the Pint after the function is finished.

Lite Raspberry Ice Cream

Prep time: 5 minutes | Cook time: 3 minutes | Serves 4

1½ cups fresh raspberries	sweetener blend
1 teaspoon freshly squeezed lemon juice	1 teaspoon raw agave nectar
¼ cup stevia–cane sugar	1 cup heavy cream

1. In a blender, combine the raspberries and lemon juice; puree until smooth. 2. Pour the raspberry and lemon mixture into a large bowl, add the stevia blend and agave nectar, and mix until well combined. Stir in the heavy cream. 3. Pour the base into a clean CREAMi Pint. Place the storage lid on the container and freeze for 24 hours. 4. Remove the pint from the freezer and take off the lid. Place the pint in the outer bowl of your Ninja CREAMi, install the Creamerizer Paddle in the outer bowl lid, and lock the lid assembly onto the outer bowl. Place the bowl assembly on the motor base, and twist the handle to the right to raise the platform and lock it in place. Select the Lite Ice Cream function. 5. Once the machine has finished processing, remove the ice cream from the pint. Serve immediately.

Mixed Berries Milkshake

Prep time: 5 minutes | Cook time: 3 minutes | Serves 2

1½ cups vanilla ice cream	½ cup fresh mixed berries
½ cup milk	

1. In an empty Ninja CREAMi pint container, place ice cream followed by milk and berries. 2. Arrange the container into the outer bowl of Ninja CREAMi. 3. Install the Creamerizer Paddle onto the lid of Outer Bowl. 4. Then rotate the lid clockwise to lock. 5. Press Power button to turn on the unit. 6. Then press Milkshake button. 7. When the program is completed, turn the Outer Bowl and release it from the machine. 8. Transfer the shake into serving glasses and serve immediately.

Chocolate Ice Cream Milkshake

Prep time: 5 minutes | Cook time: 3 minutes | Serves 1

1½ cups chocolate ice cream	½ cup whole milk

1. In an empty Ninja CREAMi pint container, place ice cream, followed by milk. 2. Arrange the container into the Outer Bowl of Ninja CREAMi. 3. Install the Creamerizer Paddle onto the lid of Outer Bowl. 4. Then rotate the lid clockwise to lock. 5. Press Power button to turn on the unit. 6. Then press Milkshake button. 7. When the program is completed, turn the Outer Bowl and release it from the machine. 8. Transfer the shake into a serving glass and serve immediately.

Lite Coffee Chip Ice Cream

Prep time: 5 minutes | Cook time: 3 minutes | Serves 4

- ¾ cup unsweetened coconut cream
- ¼ cup monk fruit sweetener with erythritol
- ½ teaspoon stevia sweetener
- 1½ tablespoons instant coffee granules
- 1 cup unsweetened rice milk
- 1 teaspoon vanilla extract
- ¼ cup low-sugar vegan chocolate chips

1. In a large bowl, whisk the coconut cream until smooth. Add the monk fruit sweetener, stevia, instant coffee, rice milk, and vanilla to the bowl; whisk until everything is well combined and the sugar is dissolved. 2. Pour the base into a clean CREAMi Pint. Place the storage lid on the container and freeze for 24 hours. 3. Remove the pint from the freezer and take off the lid. Place the pint in the outer bowl of your Ninja CREAMi, install the Creamerizer Paddle in the outer bowl lid, and lock the lid assembly onto the outer bowl. Place the bowl assembly on the motor base, and twist the handle to the right to raise the platform and lock it in place. Select the Lite Ice Cream function. 4. Use a spoon to create a 1½-inch-wide hole that goes all the way to the bottom of the pint. Pour the chocolate chips into the hole. then replace the pint lid and select the Mix-In function. 5. Once the machine has finished processing, remove the ice cream from the pint. Serve immediately.

Mocha Milkshake

Prep time: 5 minutes | Cook time: 3 minutes | Serves 2

- 1½ cups chocolate ice cream
- ½ cup cashew milk
- ½ cup ripe banana, peeled and cut into ½-inch pieces
- 1 tablespoon instant coffee powder

1. In an empty Ninja CREAMi pint container, place ice cream followed by milk, banana and coffee powder. 2. Arrange the container into the Outer Bowl of Ninja CREAMi. 3. Install the Creamerizer Paddle onto the lid of Outer Bowl. 4. Then rotate the lid clockwise to lock. 5. Press Power button to turn on the unit. 6. Then press Milkshake button. 7. When the program is completed, turn the Outer Bowl and release it from the machine. 8. Transfer the shake into serving glasses and serve immediately.

Mocha Tahini Milkshake

Prep time: 5 minutes | Cook time: 3 minutes | Serves 2

- 1½ cups chocolate ice cream
- ½ cup unsweetened oat milk
- ¼ cup tahini
- 2 tablespoons coffee
- 1 tablespoon chocolate fudge

1. In an empty Ninja CREAMi pint container, place ice cream followed by milk, tahini, coffee and fudge. 2. Arrange the container into the Outer Bowl of Ninja CREAMi. 3. Install the Creamerizer Paddle onto the lid of Outer Bowl. 4. Then rotate the lid clockwise to lock. 5. Press Power button to turn on the unit. 6. Then press Milkshake button. 7. When the program is completed, turn the Outer Bowl and release it from the machine. 8. Transfer the shake into serving glasses and serve immediately.

Baileys Milkshake

Prep time: 5 minutes | Cook time: 5 minutes | Serves 1

- 1 scoop vanilla ice cream
- 1 scoop chocolate ice cream
- 1 tablespoon chocolate sauce
- 1 tablespoon caramel sauce
- 2 fluid ounces Baileys Irish Cream
- 1 cup whole milk

1. Place all ingredients into an empty CREAMi Pint. 2. Place Pint in outer bowl, install Creamerizer Paddle onto outer bowl lid and lock the lid assembly on the outer bowl. Place the bowl assembly on the motor base and crank the lever to elevate and secure the platform in place. 3. Choose the MILKSHAKE option. 4. Remove the milkshake from the Pint after the processing is finished.

Coffee Vodka Milkshake

Prep time: 5 minutes | Cook time: 3 minutes | Serves 2

- 2 cups vanilla ice cream
- 2 tablespoons coffee liqueur
- 2 tablespoons vodka

1. In an empty Ninja CREAMi pint container, place ice cream, followed by coffee liqueur and vodka. 2. Arrange the container into the outer bowl of Ninja CREAMi. 3. Install the "Creamerizer Paddle" onto the lid of outer bowl. 4. Then rotate the lid clockwise to lock. 5. Press "Power" button to turn on the unit. 6. Then press "MILKSHAKE" button. 7. When the program is completed, turn the outer bowl and release it from the machine. 8. Transfer the shake into serving glasses and serve immediately.

Lemon Cookie Milkshake

Prep time: 8 minutes | Cook time: 3 minutes | Serves 2

- 1½ cups vanilla ice cream
- 3 lemon cream sandwich cookies
- ¼ cup milk

1. In an empty Ninja CREAMi pint container, place ice cream followed by cookies and milk. 2. Arrange the container into the Outer Bowl of Ninja CREAMi. 3. Install the Creamerizer Paddle onto the lid of Outer Bowl. 4. Then rotate the lid clockwise to lock. 5. Press Power button to turn on the unit. 6. Then press Milkshake button. 7. When the program is completed, turn the Outer Bowl and release it from the machine. 8. Transfer the shake into serving glasses and serve immediately.

Banana Milkshake

Prep time: 5 minutes | Cook time: 3 minutes | Serves 2

1 scoop vanilla ice cream

2 small bananas, peeled and halved

7 fluid ounces semi-skimmed milk

1. In an empty Ninja CREAMi pint container, place ice cream followed by bananas and milk. 2. Arrange the container into the Outer Bowl of Ninja CREAMi. 3. Install the Creamerizer Paddle onto the lid of Outer Bowl. 4. Then rotate the lid clockwise to lock. 5. Press Power button to turn on the unit. 6. Then press Milkshake button. 7. When the program is completed, turn the Outer Bowl and release it from the machine. 8. Transfer the shake into serving glasses and serve immediately.

Chocolate Ginger Milkshake

Prep time: 5 minutes | Cook time: 3 minutes | Serves 2

1½ cups chocolate ice cream

½ cup oat milk

1 teaspoon ground ginger

¼ cup chocolate, grated

1. In an empty Ninja CREAMi pint container, place the ice cream. 2. With a spoon, create a 1½-inch wide hole in the center that reaches the bottom of the pint container. 3. Add the remaining ingredients into the hole. 4. Arrange the container into the outer bowl of Ninja CREAMi. 5. Install the "Creamerizer Paddle" onto the lid of outer bowl. 6. Then rotate the lid clockwise to lock. 7. Press "Power" button to turn on the unit. 8. Then press "MILKSHAKE" button. 9. When the program is completed, turn the outer bowl and release it from the machine. 10. Transfer the shake into serving glasses and serve immediately.

Chocolate Hazelnut Milkshake

Prep time: 6 minutes | Cook time: 10 minutes | Serves 2

1 cup chocolate ice cream

½ cup whole milk

¼ cup hazelnut spread

1. Place the ice cream in an empty CREAMi Pint. 2. Create a 1½-inch-wide hole in the bottom of the Pint using a spoon. Fill the hole with the remaining ingredients. 3. Place Pint in outer bowl, install Creamerizer Paddle onto outer bowl lid and lock the lid assembly on the outer bowl. Place bowl assembly on motor base and twist the handle right to raise the platform and lock in place. 4. Select MILKSHAKE. 5. When the milkshake has finished processing, take it from the Pint and serve right away.

Made in the USA
Middletown, DE
02 May 2023